Motivational & Inspirational Poems
(For Valley Moments)

E. P. McKnight

WORDS 'N' ACTION

*To: Candice,
May you be encouraged by these words!! Your Mother wants you to feel better!!*

E.P. McKnit

WORDS 'N' ACTION

Copyright © 1996, 2007 by E. P. McKnight

All rights reserved. No part of this book may be reproduced or utilized in any form or by any means, electronic or mechanical, including photocopying, recording, or by any information storage or retrieval system without the written consent of the Publisher, except by a reviewer who may quote brief passages for review purposes.

Printed in the U.S.A.

ISBN 978-1-4303-2053-1

First Edition   1996
Second Edition 2008

Contact: Nikao Imani Productions
          nikaoimani@yahoo.com
             818 903- 5555

I dedicate this book to my Parents
Paul & Lucille Goldsmith
My inspiration and encouragement

FOREWARD

I was deeply honored and delighted to be asked to write the Forward for E.P.'s inspiring, uplifting and beautiful book of poetry, "WORDS 'N' ACTION"

I have known E.P. McKnight for about eight years. We met at a bookstore where I work and where she was doing research. I was trying to help her find what she needed. As we talked, we discovered we shared a love of acting, creativity and both had lived in New York. I was immediately drawn by her enthusiasm, energy and most important her sense of self. We have been friends ever since.

Ms. McKnight is one of the most talented people I know…she is an actress, a writer, a teacher and has an amazing ability to constantly reinvent herself, learn and grow. Through the years of knowing her and watching her in action I am always surprised, impressed and in awe of her boundless energy, determination and generosity of spirit. Her perseverance when attacking a project is remarkable…she knows no obstacle and never quits until her goals are accomplished.

I was thrilled last year to see her perform in her one-woman play "I QUESTION AMERICA: THE LEGACY OF MS. FANNIE LOU HAMER," Her stage presence and charisma in this show that she wrote, performed and produced is a tour de force. It has been her calling card as she performs and tours the country with this powerful and educational piece of work.

Her book "WORDS 'N' ACTION" is divided into eleven categories representing life. She shares so much wisdom in her words which reflect our humanity and captures our joy, pain, fears, strengths, triumphs… and most important our spirituality and the power of God, love, faith and hope. Her poems are stirring, spiritual and touch the soul.

The book is also an amazing tribute to her African American heritage and tradition while acknowledging and paying homage to God and all his Children…I am so blessed to know E.P. McKnight.

                                                                Jeanie Coggan, CA

The pain in some and the joy in others inspired me to write this collection of inspirational and motivational expression. My purpose is to provoke thought, inspire action, heal the wounded and to affect all that partake of these inspired words.

Happy is the man that findeth wisdom, and the man that getteth understanding.
                                                              Proverbs 3:13

CONTENTS

I. GOD'S OMNIPOTENT

God Don't Need No Stars	1
God, The Creator	3
God, The Liberator	4
Thank God Anyhow	5
Honor The Creator	6
Good Morning World, Good Morning God, Good Morning Self	7
Listen To Your Heart	8

II. RELATIONSHIP

Is Anybody There?	10
I Am Lonely	12
Color Me Heart	13
A Friend	14
All Is Well	15
Spiritual Exercise	16
The Aching One	17
Love Ministry	18
Perpetual	19

III. HOPE

Midnight Before Dawn	21
Truth Stands On Its Own	22
Give Thanks For Less For More	23
Dreams	24
The Answer	25
Life Is No Bed Of Roses	26
Nobody Can Turn You Around	27
There Is Room At The Top For You	28
The Examination	29
The Dove	30
The Potter's Hand	31
Tree Of Life	32

IV. SELF-ESTEEM

Press Your Way	34
Say It, Believe It and Watch It	35
Rise Up	36
Flowers	37
A Yes Time, A No Time	38
I've Got A Voice	39

V. WISDOM

Harvesting	41
Ask For What You Want	42
Arm Yourself	43
Attitude To Altitude	44
Information To Revelation	45
New Levels, New Devils	46

VI. KNOWLEDGE

MIA	48
C's To Transform Your Life	49
D's To Transform Your Life	51
L's To Transform Your Life	52
AB&C For Daily Moments	53
Beauty For Ashes	54

VII. LEGACY

A Child Shall Lead Them	55
Voices From The Village	56
Who Do You Owe?	57
Whose Gonna?	58
Youth	59

VIII. FUTURE

Destruction	62
Destiny	63
The Road To Nowhere, The Road To Somewhere	64
Fearfulness	65
Drowning	66

IX. CELEBRATION

The Gathering	68
Reflection	70
The Trailblazers	71
Visions And Dreams	73
Forerunners	74
Thanksgiving	75
Accommodation	77
Acquaintanceship	78
A Majesty For All Seasons	80
Warriors	81
Faithful Ambassador	83
Commemoration	84
Lasting Impression	85
The Veteran	86
The Union	88
Mother's Day, A Rose	90
Father's Day, A Root	92

XII. AVOCATION

The Praiser	95
One Race, One Prize	96
The Called	97
The Giver	98
Don't Count Me Out	99
The Fiery Furnace	100
The Greeting Kiss	101

\

XII. AMERICAN HISTORY

Mrs. Fannie Lou Hamer, The Majorette	103
Dr. Martin Luther King Jr., The Drum Major	105
Mrs. Rosa Parks, The Innovator	107
Mrs. Victoria Adams, A True Champion	108
The Flavor Of The Universe	109
Footsteps	111
African Americans	113
Daredevil Of The Sky	115
Tuskegee Airmen-Righting The Wrong	116
Leonard Hicks, The Ultimate Giver	117

I.   GOD'S OMNIPOTENT

Words 'N' Action

"In the beginning God created the heaven and earth." (Genesis 1:1).

God Don't Need No Stars

According to the book of Genesis
The beginning of time, our nemesis
God created heaven and earth all by himself
Placing all things on his designed mantelshelf
All the planets, stars, Pluto and Mars
God Don't Need No Stars.

In six days, he created all
With his power, he did call
Man, woman and the universe
With his divine power
To spring forth at the divine hour.

He did not have one star
Not one near or far
Until he created man and woman, Adam & Eve
Not following instructions, he was grieved
Because of Satan, God got stars
From good and evil, came many wars.

There is Adam who lost focus on God's instruction
Not paying attention, caused much destruction
And Eve who was so easily distracted and persuaded
Before her an apple was presented, and paraded
They made decisions based on their own intellect and emotions
This caused much strife, grief and a great commotion
Adam and Eve error, was indeed five star
Still reeking havoc and pain, around thus far.

Today, in churches
The same spirit lurches
The Adams' and Eves' have become so star struck
Consuming and affecting, like a big Mack truck
Even the mega churches cannot contain them
From being a stumbling block, much mayhem.

Words 'N' Action

From the pulpit to the pews
Constantly breaking the rules
These stars glow is almost blinding
Glittery, shinning and stinging
Too often causing disharmony, wars
Note, God Don't Need No Stars.

God is God all by himself
Needing nothing, no one else
Creations designed for God's glorification
Admiration, honor and our dedication.

All you stars that is glowing out there
You're all around and solidly everywhere
First wipe off the shine from your face
Begin anew in a better space
Have a little talk with God
Read the Word, his golden rod
Will make things right
No effort, not even a fight
Then you will know who the real star is
Because God Don't Need No Stars.

"And God made the firmament Heaven, and divided the waters..." (Genesis 1:7).

God, The Creator

God, the divine, due the credit
Many admit and truly admire it
About all creations, its wonderment
Concurring, chiding with adornment
Look at the stars, the sun, the moon
None was created a moment too soon
Even begun time, night and day
Illuminating man's path, show the way.

Only God can allow procreation
Joining the sperm, the egg, in formation
Often man seeks to engineer this process
Trying to clone, reproduce, but digress
For lack of control over life and death
Not even near to creating one's breath
Only the Creator has this power
All others have failed and soured.

God created the human computer, the brain
Giving us five senses to educate and train
No batteries or electrical impulses required
Just his spirit, within us reside
When you awake in the morning
Be thankful and not bemoaning
The movement of your limbs, your energy
Your thoughts, with precise synergy
All things within functioning on time
All in harmony as life goes and chimes
God, Creator, Allah, Jehovah, many names
Nevertheless over humankind, he yet reigns
No matter the name, he's still in control
The World he spins and let it roll
God, the same yesterday, today, forever
For a better life, seek and endeavor.

"So that we may boldly say The Lord is my helper, and I will not fear..." (Hebrews 13:6).

God, The Liberator

Each day you allow, created me be
Grant me wisdom, spiritual eye to see
Clear the path, you designed me to tread
A soldier like John the Baptist, nothing I dread
Just crying in the wilderness, for all to seek
Making a mighty difference, but yet so meek
Grant me courage like Esther, who stood firm
You granted her favor, as she waited her turn
Even Jeremiah was determined, his house on fire
With passion flowing thru and a strong desire
To alert all, of the one true Messiah
Righteousness took Ruth down an unknown path
She endured, married wealthy, you do the math
Grant me the faith of Job, that held on tight
Through tears, anguish, he emerged all right
Walking by faith and not by sight
Believing God got his back just right
Commitment like Deborah, to fight the mighty war
Against demonic angelic beings, and winning by far
And be as wise as Solomon, for all the world to know
God's the lamp unto your feet, each step as you go
Humbleness as a child, committing all to you
Knowing eventually the answer will come through
Loving all can cause the heart much pain
But with agape love, and God will surely reign
While I be, my brother and sister's keeper
Making my joy within go deeper and deeper
Exemplifying love, joy, peace, to attest
Long-suffering, goodness, faith, the rest
As I fight this battle, this very day
To hear my Savior eventually say,
 "Well done my good and faithful servant."

"In every thing give thanks: for this is the will of God..." (1 Thessalonians 5:18).

Thank God Anyhow

When the roof of your home seems like its caving in on you
And the walls appear to be closing in like the morning dew
The floor seems to be quite rocky, all so unstable
Thank God Anyhow, and know he's able.

Take a quiet moment, remember when times were better
Know this is just a mere season, you must weather
Your castle will resume, every room filled with joy
Washing away all tears with a bright convoy.

God brought you through those times
Be a testament, let your light shine
While God works, just stand still
Let God be God, doing his will.

After reflecting and thanking God for his grace
Step out on faith, believe, you win the race
Blessings of yesterday, today's testament
God deemed all, for your betterment.

Thank God Anyhow
He puts no more on you than you can bare
Humble yourself, cast your cares, leave it there
He will eventually set you free
Free to thank him, wait and see
Just serve him, let all things be
No matter what, Thank God Anyhow.

"...the only wise God, be honour and glory for ever and ever. Amen." (1 Timothy 1:17).

Honor the Creator

The words of God come to teach
Inform, direct, support, reach
Penetrate and the list goes on
Like an old hymnal song.

God's words in theory are fine
Application makes the difference in time
Affirmation of God's manifestation, comes true
Touching your soul, adhering like glue.

Some stomp, dance, clap, wave
Tears flowing, singing, witness to others, they're saved
However you praise, it is your route
The Spirit within, surrounds you about.

You should honor the Creator, for he is worthy to be praised
Honoring him with praise and thanksgiving, all your days
Honoring him, in the end you truly win
He is alpha, omega, beginning and the end.

"Thou hast granted me life and favour,...." (Job 10:12).

Good Morning World, Good Morning God, Good Morning Self

Today, I will work harder than yesterday
For tomorrow is not promised, anyway
I will love others more than yesterday
For today is all I have, I dare say
I will give more today than any other day
For this day will never come again, gone away
I will make this moment the best yet
For this moment is mine to be, no fret
I ask God to be the head of my life
For without God there is much strife
I will share love with the world
And the world will share love with me
God plus me is the majority
I will love myself harder each day
For God gives and God taketh away
Each morning when I awake
My eyes open, for my sake
God gives me life another moment,
Another day, with permission he consents
I say, "Good Morning World
Good Morning God
Good Morning Self
For it is great to be alive
And to God I strive."

"Hear, O my people, and I will speak;..." (Psalm 50:7).

Listen To Your Heart

Today is a new day in my life
Yet, today seems very much like yesterday
The day before and the day before that.

As I look back, all my days resemble
There has got to be a better day
As I sit and look at all creation
I wonder, "what is my purpose?"

A quiet, still, gentle, crystal clear voice spoke to me saying,
"Listen to your heart"
"Listen to your heart", I thought.

While pondering and being bewildered
The same quiet, gentle voice repeated
"Listen To Your Heart. Allow me to enter
Do not shut me out
Rely on me
All your cares, needs and wants
May be fulfilled but you must first listen to your heart."

I thought, "Who is that? God is that you?
If it is you, then make this day different from all my other days"
Then God said, "Listen To Your Heart. I already did
But you must first Listen To Your Heart."

II. RELATIONSHIP

"......I will never leave thee, nor forsake thee." (Hebrew 13:5).

Is Anybody There?

Dear church, hear my voice
I sit next to you, my heart aches with pain
It feels as if the next beat may be my last
Hear my cry!

I look to my left, you're jumping up and down
I look to my right, you're dozing
I look forward, no one sees me
I look behind me
I am invisible to those that look ahead.

Oh, Church, hear my cry!
Don't you see me? My pain?
Help! Stop! Look! Listen! Help!

I stay away from church, no one calls
Sickness in my family, not a call or card
A word of encouragement, my heart cries out
Church? Is Anybody There? Hear my cry!

I am your sister, your brother
Your missionary, your minister
Your deacon, your deaconess
Your usher, I am.

Oh Church, hear my cry!
Heed my voice
From north, south, east or west
A kind word, a phone call, a prayer.

Is Anybody There?
Knock and the doors shall be open
Seek and you shall find
Ask and it shall be given to you.

Words 'N' Action

Oh Church, I am seeking, knocking and asking
God uses our hands and feet
When I seek, do not look the other way
When I knock, do not close the door
When I ask, do not tell me, "God is able and walk away"
Oh Church! Hear my cry! Is Anybody There?

"Every man's work shall be made manifest:...." (1 Corinthians 3:13).

I'm Lonely

Sitting in a dismal room
No one to talk with, I feel so alone
Worthless, no one cares
I asked, "God, millions of people in creation
And no one to hear me or care, how could this be?"
God replied, "My child, how can you be lonely?
I made you one of the most unique creatures in the universe
You have a talent that only you can do. You must seek it out
Look around you. There is none other like you
Though there are millions of you, male and female
From sea to sea, to every corner of the world
There is so much that could be done
Needs to be done and should be done
How can you be lonely?

Loneliness is cured with love
You were created out of love
You must love everybody, male and female
Love each other and help each other
Work with each other and encourage each other
Share with each other and compliment each other
Support each other.

My child, how can you be lonely?
Today, did you take time to say I love you to someone
Your neighbor, a friend, mother, father, relative or child?
Did you help the needed?
Did you spend a moment encouraging the down-trodden?
Did you share a kind word with a passerby?
Did you do anything to make this world a better place to live
For yourself and others?
Are you not doing what I created you to do?
Your loneliness is by choice and it is not good to be alone.

"This is my commandment, That ye love one another, as I have loved you." (John 15:12).

Color Me Heart

When I am not what you want me to be, Color Me Heart
When I am the best that I can be, Color Me Heart
When I am the worst you think yet, Color Me Heart.

Color Me Heart, and not black, when you do not understand me
Color Me Heart, and not green with envy, when you desire what I have
Color Me Heart, and not red with fear, because of our differences
Color Me Heart, and not pink with joy, when I am down and out
Color Me Heart, and not blue with the blues because you are feeling low
Color Me Heart, and not white to pretend I do not exist and am invisible.

Color Me Heart, with love so that we may live in harmony
Harmony in our homes, communities, schools, government and world
If you Color Me Heart, we can walk shoulder to shoulder
Hand in hand and side by side
Peace on earth for all humankind
It is so simple, just Color Me Heart.

"......and there is a friend that sticketh closer than a brother." (Proverb 18:24).

A Friend

A true friend comes along once in a lifetime or maybe twice
So called friends pass through like tidal waves
They go with the flow
When things are good they are paramount
When things are not so good, they disappear like the wind.

A true friend stays with you through thick and thin
A true friend accepts you the way you are
A true friend never demands to know
But lifts you up during your weakest moment
Turns your frown into a smile, forgives without a request
And does not tire of your endless cries
But dries every tear.

When your path seem lonely and desolate
A friend walks side by side with you
Supporting you with strength, love and caring
A true friend makes the impossible seem possible
When you stumble and fall, a true friend lifts you and
Says, "Hold on, you can do it, keep the faith."

True friends apart, are bound by the heart
You often think on each other with fondness and comfort
True friends are bound by spirit and soul.

"I am Alpha and Omega, the beginning and the ending,..."(Revelation 1:8).

All Is Well

Believe that All Is Well
Within you God dwells
If you say you can do it
God will take you through it
He is what you need him to be
He is what will set you free
From A to Z, he is your:
    A-Advocator and Ambassador
    B-Battle Fighter, Bishop and Balancer
    C-Creator, Comforter and Caretaker
    D-Deliverer, Decision Maker, Doctor and Director
    E-Earner, Empire and Edifier
    F-Father, Feeder and Forgiver
    G-Great God, Giver and Guide
    H-Healer, Helper and Hope
    I-Illuminator, Instructor and Intercessor
    J-Joy, Justifier and Judge
    K-Keeper
    L-Leader, Lawyer and Lord
    M-Maker, Mantle, Master, Mediator and Messiah
    N- Nurturer and Nourisher
    O-Omnipotent and omnipresent God
    P-Peace-maker, Physician and Purifier
    Q-Quieter
    R-Redeemer, Reformer, Revealer, Rewarder and Ruler
    S-Saviour, Sanctifier, Security, Shepherd and Spirit
    T-Teacher, Tester and Tower of strength
    U-Universal God, Uniter and Up righter
    V-Victor, vigilant and virtuous
    W-Way maker, Warrior and Watch Tower
    Y-Yahweh
    Z-Zealousness
God can be whatever you need
When, where, believe and proceed.

"But grow in grace, and in the knowledge of our Lord and Saviour..." (II Peter 3:18).

Spiritual Exercise

Working out, good for the mind, body and soul
Releasing stress, losing weight, the young and old
All kinds of ills from your body, you eliminate
Feeling fit, thinking clear and looking great.

Trials and testings, require Spiritual Exercise
Meditate on God's Word daily, you will rise
Spiritual Exercise requires preparation
It begins with the one who designed creation
Guidance, truth and wisdom, yours for the asking
Feed your spirit, enjoy life everlasting
Surround yourself with positive, caring and spiritual people
All in all, makes you weather storms like a well built steeple.

With Spiritual Exercise, you're a warrior in combat
You stand firmly, battle down, the adversary you sat
With Spiritual Exercise, your enemy will quickly flee
Victory belongs to God, and you're now set free.

Your hand in the Creator's hand, he is the overseer
More Spiritual Exercise, he makes all things clearer
The more equipped, friends and family, you intercede
You will lessen their pain, diminishing there greed.

"....And the woman was made whole from that hour." (Matthew 9:22).

The Aching One

There once was this lady who always desired to be heard
She had a lot to say but, never uttered a word
Years passed, she remained silent
Inwardly, was torn, twisted and bent.

She fought one day to speak her piece
Anger poured from her lips, it did not cease
Tears stained her eyes, pain conquered her heart
Grief blurred her words, each time she would start.

Anger and grief, from an insult many years ago.
Wounded so deep, caused a nose bleed so
Agonizing over the past, she traveled around
Seeking solace, relief, no help abound.

Desperately seeking help, escape, be pain free
She cried aloud, "God please help me,
Remove this bitter cup from my breast"
Everywhere I go, I find no rest
Some days, death looks mighty good
But my desire to live, within me stood.

A moment of peace I know not
No one else, God you're all I got
To forgive, I must, to be free
So this pain, anger, grief to flee
Forgiveness, I know, now is the key
I must do, thou soul to be set free.

"Love worketh no ill to his neighbor;..." (Romans 13:10).

Love Ministry

We must minister in love one to another
For love is of the Creator and no other
They who love must love like the Creator
Form a relationship with him sooner or later
If you know not the Creator, you know not agape love
All good things flow from the Heavens above.

Love with all your heart, your neighbor as yourself
Ministering with love to each other, and nothing else
Your ministry may be to teach, with love teach
Your ministry may be to preach, with love preach
As a pastor, your charge for others, lead like a dove
All working together for good, no strife, no shove.

If you want love, give love, you won't thirst
You want people to love you, love them first
You want people to respect you, respect too
Compliment others, and compliment to you due

Agape love permits you to love the unlovable
To serve the unservable, forgive the unforgivable
Love the addict, alcoholic, liar and prostitute, alike
Pick that person up out of the pit, even from the dike
The broken and beaten, restore with a gentle touch
That wounded soul, kind words, means so much
Make the difference, with Agape love you give
Making the world a better placed to be and live.

"A friend loveth at all times,..." (Proverbs 17:17).

Perpetual

When I come to meet and see you
It's like being refreshed by morning dew
Then I see that loving smile
Makes me want to stay awhile
People like you make the world so bright
Making our visit, spiritual and out of sight
Heartfelt blessings comes to wish you God's best
As you approach life's journey and all the rest!!!
Know in my heart, memories of you remain
Knowing you, I will be forever change
Because you make the difference, like day and night
My friend, near or far, we will always be tight
This will forever remain, neither death can change
For in my heart, memories and joys forever reign.

III. HOPE

"Knowing this, that the trying of your faith worketh patience." (James 1:3).

Midnight Before Dawn

Sometimes our troubles, tribulations seem more than we can bear
Our days appear to be dreary, dark as midnight, while our heart's tear
Wondering, "Why me? Why not someone else?" as the story goes
Everyone experiences pains, some hide it, while others let it show.

Without failure, if we change our perspective on our situation
Or if we compare our situation with another's, degradation
Somehow our situation is not as bad as it seems
All is just for a season, as God has this day deemed.

For without darkness, there can be no light
Without pain and suffering, no appreciation when all is right
Experiencing the true feeling of joy and happiness is a gift
For God has removed the pain, and your burden, he lift
Without experiences, maturity may never be
Without midnight, to the dawn, you never see.

Words 'N' Action

"Truth shall spring out of the earth;..."(Psalm 85:11).

Truth Stands On Its Own

During this dispensation, the wrongs appear to be right
The rights are wrong; this is our common day plight
Families are becoming total strangers, much apart
Broken by strife, anger, issues, hidden in the dark.

All that was once good now seem to be horribly bad
Immorals have replaced morals, some gone mad
Many have a hard time, great effort to smile
Stares and frowns, run rampant down the isles.

In the mirror, that face staring back, unfamiliar to you
What happened, suddenly life changed, you did too
Nothing seems to be right, life, a horn in your side
Your feel like a prisoner, with strong chains you tide
 Nowhere to turn, and inwardly you churn.

First, sit down take a long look at reality
Look at the truth in your life, its' legality
The only way to begin again, begin with the truth
The truth always stands on its own, like a root
The truth will set you free, all else will flee.

Determine the truth that got you in this mess
Focusing on the truth, will exonerate you at best
Defining your problem, solutions at the door await
The truth always stands on its' own, just reach and take
It awaits your discovery of it, it waits to free you
It allows you to begin anew, as you beam through
It may hurt initially, but in time it will heal
If you allow it too, receive from God, the best deal.

"........*in whatsoever state I am, there-with to be content.*" *(Philippians 4:11).*

Give Thanks For Less For More

Spending energy complaining about what you have not
Should be spent thanking the Creator for what you've got
No matter how mediocre, insignificant or small
Tomorrow's blessings may supersede, cure all.

The small or insignificant, show your appreciation
You never know what awaits you at the next station
Five thousands were fed with five loaves, two fishes
Surely God clearly knows and sees your desires, wishes.

True appreciation deeply within your soul, your current state
Be contented, thanking the Creator, your blessings await
Stand still and believe, know that all is well
Give Thanks For Less For More, listen for Heaven's bell.

"Both riches and honour come of thee, and thou reignest over all;"(1 Chronicles 29:12).

Dreams

Dreams are the substance of hopes, desires and wishes
You may dream a dream for a week, month, or even a year
But no matter what, in order for that dream to materialize
You must wake up, spiritually and naturally, even through tears.

Too often people speak of yesterday's dreams
Dreams cannot and do not manifest themselves
Once you are aware of your dream you must act
Else it becomes just a dream, on which you sat.

The Creator has given you all the tools of power
To make your dreams come true, the destined hour
The power that brings change and new life
Shake off the negative, put on the positive
Be on the winning side, with God as your guide
Radiate a smile when things are not the greatest
Combating depression, disease, pain and affliction
Maturity in God, allows you triumph with any situation
No matter the circumstances or the duration
You only have to tap your spirituality within
Allow this power to flow from within, and begin
Dreams become reality when you act, and stay on track.

"Delight thyself also in the lord; and he shall give thee the desires of thine heart."
(Psalm 37:4).

The Answer

The Creator has all the answers
The Creator is The Answer
Honoring the Creator in your life makes the difference
Letting go and letting the God will change your life
The Creator is always sensitive to your needs
Whereas people are not necessarily, but he will heed
The Creator will deliver you from whatever your condition
Showing you the best way of life, a new rendition.

You were given eyes to behold miracles and wonders
A tongue, a heart to fellowship with, sending praises a yonder
Ears to hear, God as your guide, through intuition he bides.

With faith, with a doubt you can make it
Use your senses, work, and act, don't sit
Allow the Creator to see you through the good and bad
But you must believe, and follow him like the little lad.

"That ye be not slothful, but followers of them who through faith and patience..."
(Hebrews 6:12).

Life Is No Bed Of Roses

Life is filled with ups and downs
Roses and thorns, all around
Promises are made, promises are broken
Promises give hope, flatter the heart
Make the spirit grow fonder, as you start.

Filled promises make you glad
With excitement, joy, you've never had
Unfulfilled promises can make you rage
With disappointment, locked in a cage.

People, inevitably, will make promises that cannot be kept
But the Creator never makes a promise which cannot be kept
Stretch forth with faith on the Creator's promises, and step
You only have to ask, look for, watch
God's path will take you up a notch
The Creator's omnipotence makes it so
He's omnipresence and ready to go.

Be not like Abraham and Sarah in Genesis
They doubted the Creator's promise of a son
In their old age, this promise was kept and beyond
The Creator may not fulfill the promise when you expect
But be assured it will be fulfilled right on time, you can bet
Keep the faith, stay focused, learn the lesson
Move ahead as you prepare for a blessing.

"But they that wait upon the Lord shall renew their strength; they shall mount up with wings as eagles..."(Isaiah 40:31).

Nobody Can Turn You Around

No matter how bad things appear, do not get turned around
The break of day is peering; the morning light is beginning to shine
Don't turn around, this season will pass, and all will be fine
You may weep at night but joy will come in the morning
Stand firmly with all your might, new hope is dawning.

The adversary may attack you in dreams, meditation
Or during your weakest moment, adding frustration
Let nothing or no one turn you around without your consent
Look backwards for strength for today, don't lament
Look forward, forge ahead, stay straight, not bent.

Sickness, heartbreak and conflicts are avenues
For the adversary to distract and misuse
Stand firmly on your beliefs and your faith
And know who's in control, standing at the gate
God's hand forcing the adversary to flee
Because there is a power within you, just plea.

"A man's gift maketh room for him, and bringeth him before great men." (Proverbs 18:16).

There is Room At The Top For You

Whatever is destined for you, you will get it
No matter how off the path you get, don't quit
No matter how the distance seems unattainable
No matter what people say, know God is able
No matter how circumstances appear to the contrary
No matter how crowded the path, there is room for you
Whatever the Creator has deemed, it will be your due.

The Creator gives you talent to glorify, honor him
Your talent will make room for you, surpassing grim
No one can take your place, but you must use what you have
Your path has been carved for you, this you can salve
A specific path to each is given, just as sure as he is risen.

Each day, build from yesterday, close the door
Welcome today with renewed faith, energy, as you soar
Go forth with fresh oil, light your lantern, follow your lead
With determination, persistence, be omnipotent, plant your seed
Within you have the power, use it every minute, every hour.

"……he will not forsake thee, neither destroy thee, nor forget the covenant of thy fathers…"(Deuteronomy 4:31).

The Examination

Some days feels like all has broken through
Reeking havoc within your soul, like hell do
All that once was, now no longer be
You feel like Job, tomorrow you can't see
All that God gave, much and more
Somehow, some reasons, flew out the door
Did I bring this upon myself, without knowing?
My fellowman, did I not assist his growing
Loving my neighbor, this commandment I kept
But yet after all my good deeds, I feel inept
With tears flowing down my heart and face
Feeling like nothing, this pain, can erase
I seek God; my cries appear to go unheard
Death in my soul, is now my favorite word
My cries so loud, my voice no longer strong
The anguish within me, what did I do wrong
Days, time is passing, tomorrow I dread
There nothing I can do, but remain instead
God hear me, remove this horrible pain
Your will I seek, as I call on your name
Ease from this anguish, is all I ask
Speak your word, I'll do the task
So that I may begin my life again at rest
To pass this stage, not repeat the test
At I mature in your word, to someday be
All the goodness you created within me.

"Likewise the Spirit also helpeth our infirmities..." (Romans 8:26).

The Dove

Sitting by the window, all is very dark
Can't see light, not even a spark
No hope, life is just passing me by
I feel like death, my fate belie
A glimmer of something my soul seek
Storms and rain, has torn me apart
No strength, no desire to restart
Oh how I wish, The Dove, is coming
Bringing new life to death, I'm humming
Loud to be heard, the raven will see
And stop by and save poor little ole me.

"Nay, in all these things we are more than conquerors ..." (Romans 8:37).

The Potter's Hand

Spinning is motion, and motion is sowing
Planting is reaping, and reaping is seeing
Seeing is believing and believing is faith
That all will work, just you see and wait
If you get what you seek, note it's God
If you don't, note it's God's testing rod
If you get that job, it's God's desire
If you don't, it's yet God, don't tire
Blessings to come, God knows how to spin
Directing your path and surely you will win
As you mature, God gets the best of your life
Through trials, tribulations, even through strife
Know you're the best, God's vessel of clay
As he works your life, molding you his way
No greater place to be, than in The Potter's Hand
Your blessings will appear, just wait and stand.

"Hope deferred maketh the heart sick; but when the desire cometh, it is a tree of life."
(Proverbs 13:12).

Tree Of Life

Hope renewed is like a tree of life,
Seeking God path removes all strife
Ordained things happen, easy flowing
Rewards unfolds without your knowing
That whatever you earnestly seek
Is already awaiting, just be meek
For no good things will be withheld
Knowing your fate is not for sale
Instilled within, your talent at birth
Waiting to enhance your part of the earth
With love and care, about you girth
Making a difference, embrace your worth
Keeping hope alive, is your destiny
Recreating life for all humanity.

Hope deferred makes the heart sick
Tearing and beating with every lick
Taking hold of your desire to try
Rejection you feel a dessert all dry
No ambitions desire or hope to be
All the time hopelessness you see
Everything through your eyes are bleak
Causing you to sit and not even seek
Much rejection has you sick, the mind is torn
Unless you do, forever your destiny's gone
Trying maybe hard, but remaining is dead
Unless you do something, your life is dread
Take one step, two steps, it ain't so bad
You may find something you never had
Hope renewed is your choice to make
At least try it, to your destiny it will take
But hope differed makes you cease to live
Disliking your life, and refusing to give
Without hope, regret, tomorrow you see.

IV. SELF-ESTEEM

"For we walk by faith, not by sight:" (II Corinthians 5:7).

Press Your Way

Whatever your endeavor, be tenacious
Whatever you do, do it with tenacity
Whatever your belief, believe tenaciously
 If you are a Christian, be a tenacious Christian
Whatever your belief, be persistent.

To be tenacious you must learn to always Press Your Way
Press Your Way through trials, for there is value in trials
No trials, no testimony, no spiritual or mental growth
No testimony, no witness, no testing, no victory
No conflict, no strength gained, no staying power.

For victory, you got to be tenacious
Conflict and trials build strength
Reserve that strength, for life's rainfall
The sun will not always shine
Hold your peace; be steadfast, unmovable and grounded.

Do not allow the rain to steal your joy
Learn to rejoice in your present state
God's grace is sufficient, his mercy endures forever
He never leads, where his grip can't keep you, press.

Prayer and wisdom are essential for the tenacious
Do not request the mountain be moved, but the strength to climb
Do not be double-minded, you are unstable, you can't win
Your reward is your deliverance, a closer relationship with thee.

Press Your Way, you can make it, your reward is awaiting you
Remain steadfast in God's word, day and night, and be true
Tenacity with God, makes the darkness light and your trials right
Whatever, be tenacious and Press Your Way, be still and stay.

"....If thou canst believe, all things are possible to him that believeth." (St. Mark 9:23).

Say It, Believe It and Watch

Goals, dreams, hopes and desires don't just occur
You must act, verbally affirm or things remain as they were
Have faith in your affirmation, say aloud
Believe in yourself, all things are possible, be proud
God has endowed you with all the tools you need
Within you he has planted your purpose, seed
Say It, Believe It and Watch.

Deeply embedded in your soul, yearnings burning like fire
Keeping your sights, thoughts, actions, don't tire
Enjoy the trip to your destination, your soul make
Time spent worthwhile, the journey makes.

Rocky roads sometimes, keep the faith, hold on tighter
When the distance seems insurmountable, be a fighter
Step by step, if you fall, fall forward, get up
Continue on, let nothing, no one interrupt.

During the rocky ride, quiet and be
Use the power of the Word, decree
Turn up faith, works, fasting, a notch
"Say It, Believe It and Watch."

"In all thy ways acknowledge him, and he shall direct thy paths." (Proverbs 3:6).

Rise Up

Rise Up from your coffin of setbacks
Grief, sickness, pain, disappointment, lack
With faith, speak victory over the occasion
Know all things don't just happen, and reason.

Rise Up to the occasion, don't get weary
Seek answers from within, without, query
You may stumble and fall, but Rise Up
These are just life's little interrupts.

Rise Up with your head held high
With your shoulders erect, don't sigh
Be proud as a peacock, and learn your way
Stride with pride, dignity, this maybe your day.

Rise Up with a new attitude, like never before
Be prepared and ready, walk through your door
God's spirit, gleaming through and through.

Rise to the occasion and the occasion will rise with you
Stay down with the occasion and the occasion wilts too
Tears flow like a running river, be distress, not defeated
You may be distressed but do not be defeated
Be cast down, not destroyed, stick around
You can beat it.

Shake the dust off your shoes, gird with righteousness, truth and honor
Rise like the sunshine, bright and gleaming, like a true marathoner
Rise Up, rise and do not look back
Go forth, like a true quarterback.

"And he gave some, apostles; and some, prophets; and some, evangelists; and some pastors and teachers;" (Ephesians 4:11).

Flowers

People are like flowers. Some bloom and some do not
Some change from season to season, spinning non stop
Week to week, month to month or year to year, they bloom
As long as there is life, change will make room.

Some may wither like weeds, others may blossom like roses
Some flowers wither from lack of moisture, small doses
People wither from lack of ambition, motivation and hope
While others bloom from season to season, grabbing every rope.

In the spring, the bloomers with accomplishments stand tall
In the winter, they seem to be well grounded, heeding their call
The harvest is plenteous but the laborers are few
What you fertilize in the winter will sprout when due.

You have choices, only the strong will survive
Use your time wisely, don't you jive
You may choose to blossom like roses, where you stand
Or wither like weeds, dying in the sand.

The power to be or not to be lies in your domain
Use your tools, champion your game
There are teachers, guides all around
Seek within, without, you will be astound
To bloom like flowers, or not to bloom is your quest
The decision is yours and all the rest.

"To every thing there is a season, and a time to every purpose under the heaven:"
(Ecclesiastes 3:1).

A Yes Time, A No Time

There is a time to live, a time to die
A time to laugh, a time to cry
A Yes Time, A No Time, don't ask why.

To all things there is a season, a time
To every purpose, the universe will chime
Knowledge, wisdom and experience will teach
A Yes Time, A No Time, don't you screech.

A yes is equally important as a no
Each has its own purpose, as you go
Each can make us or break your stride
But it all depends on your reception during the tide
How you react, respond determines your state
The choice is yours, don't wait to late.

There are only two ways to accept a yes or no
Positively or negatively, as you grow
If positive, apply to your life for growth, move on
If negative, learn the reason, good or bad, let it be gone
As long as you live, there will always be A Yes Time, A No Time
Just take the journey, do your best, stay the course, all will be fine.

"So that we may boldly say, The Lord is my helper...." (Hebrews 13:6).

I've Got A Voice

I may be a child, but I've Got A Voice
I may be little, but I've Got A Voice
I may be big, but I've Got A Voice
I may be young, but I've Got A Voice
I may be an adolescent, but I've Got A Voice
I may be timid, and I've Got A Voice
I may be shy, but I've Got A Voice
I may have a speech problem, but I've Got A Voice
No matter what, I've Got A Voice.

A voice to use to the best of my ability
For the good of myself and others' mobility
Use it to the truth I speak,
Helping, teaching others, when they seek
Like my mother, father, sister, brother
I must use it to share love with others
To bring love, joy, peace
Erasing strife, and ills to cease
Honor my elders, my past
Triumphant them, first not last
I praise God for the power to get
As I follow his covenant, I beget
I stand tall; speak bold, for I am somebody
Hear my voice, young and old, I maybe your antibody
My voice through it God may lead
Many good things, wonders and deeds.

V. WISDOM

"And some fell on good ground, and did yield fruit that sprang up and increased..." (St. Mark 4:8).

Harvesting

Nothing from nothing leaves nothing, a bore
Something plus something is something more.

When you harvest bountifully, you reap bountifully
When you harvest sparingly, you reap sparingly
When you harvest begrudgingly, your reaping is begrudge
When you harvest happily, happily you reap, don't budge.

Harvesting is a life long process, grab hold and search
You may harvest on your job, in your home, your church
With a neighbor or stranger, do what you can, just start
Whatever you do, always remember the Creator sees your heart.

What you harvest and how you harvest, you will reap
The venue may look rocky, frustrating, with faith leap
Let not inner turmoil cause you to fear
Seek help from far and near
The harvest is plenteous but the laborers are few
Do what you need, rewards sprout, you never knew.

"And whatsoever ye shall ask in my name, that will I do,..." (St. John 14:13).

Ask For What You Want

Too often afraid people don't ask, don't get
Strangling themselves in a pity net
A sneer or a frown, makes you torn
Feeling rejection, you want to run
Whatever your fear is, get over it
Otherwise in despair you sit.

There is no harm in being apprehensive
Don't remain, dismiss and live
Take a step, a miracle may appear
Awaiting to bring a hope so near
In this life, no one makes it alone
Ask For What You Want, listen for the tone
A no, is only for today
Tomorrow, maybe a yes to stay.

Not asking will, inevitably, leave you void and wanting
Like a recurring nightmare, everyday you haunting
You struggle, you fight to no avail
Defeat your foolish pride, Ask For What You Want
Get out of that drowning well
And sooner or later you will be gallant.

"Wherefore take unto you the whole armour of God, that ye may be able to withstand..."
(Ephesians 6:13).

Arm Yourself

Life is a series of battles and wars
Of joblessness, loneliness, leaving scars
Godlessness, sickness, depression, add to the strain
Defeats and setbacks, so many remain
But triumphs and victories can raise the lame.

The wars and battles do not matter
Solutions in you heart, you must chatter
With the armor of truth, righteousness, peace and faith
Will eventually win and overtake.

Arm yourself daily before the attacks
With knowledge, truth, faith, strength, you pack
To withstand the unexpected vices of the adversary
Stand firmly on faith, be in your sanctuary
For a house built with brick will stand
Gird with the Word, or your house blows like sand.

"…..they shall mount up with wings as eagles; they shall run and not be weary; and they shall walk, and not faint." (Isaiah 40:31).

Attitude To Altitude

Your every thought has much power
Changing your destiny, a given hour
Positive or negative, have an effect
Causing your destiny to go, or wreck
Believing and doing you can attain
With the actions, flowing like rain
Sit and wait nothing this make
Do something good for your sake
Will power and determination are the key
Changing your life, circumstances eventually
Believing and seeking, effects your attitude
Jumping hurdles, determines your altitude
Great attitude, wonders your journey make
Being unstoppable, success your destiny takes
God has given you the power to accomplish
It's not easy, but he will fulfill every wish
According to his purpose, and his plan
For your life, so seek and just stand.

"Happy is the man that findeth wisdom, and the man that getteth understanding." (Proverbs 3:13).

Information Is Revelation

Seeking the Word, God then speaks
God's assured, you must seek
God's grace overcomes doubt
His love and kindness all about
Use your God kind of faith
Plan your day, don't you wait
Through wisdom, the process endure
Each step of the way, your faith mature
Be in the spirit, a day of fasting
Benefits gotten, sure and everlasting
Through knowledge, the process endure
God's promises, most definite for sure
Praying, fasting, studying and waiting
Does spiritual wonders, while creating
Choose to forgive, your heart clean
Love completely, don't be mean
Giving and receiving, a fact of life
Ensures God's blessings, airtight
Seeing is believing, check the book
The Bible and others, have a look.

"Knowing this, that the trying of your faith worketh patience." (James 1:3).

New Levels, New Devils

Being blessed is a good thing
Just know Satan waits in the wing
Trying to trip and make you stray
From all that's good, to be taken away
When troubles, on your shoulders mount
Illness and grief, seems paramount
Count it all joy, God stands in the wing
Awaiting your cry and to him you sing
Satan is no challenge for the best
Take comfort in faith, and be at rest
Circumstances often make you fear
Be still and listen, God's voice to hear
Directions will come your way
Just be still and don't you stray
New Levels, New Devils, only for a season
And know, God allows all for a reason
Soon all this will soon past
Nothing is forever and forever last
Except for the Word of God
Guiding you with a gentle rod
Allowing the new devils, it's just a test
New levels, more blessings & all the rest!

VI. KNOWLEDGE

"Blessed is the man that endureth temptation: for when he is tried, he shall receive the crown of life,.." (James 1: 12).

MIA

Each day, life filled with constant learning
Our little brain busy in class and churning
When one least expect, the teacher gives a test
Making you examine life and see its best
While determine the rules for the day
Pounding away, each step of the way
Seeking answers from above,
None to be heard, quite as a dove
You wonder why God's so still
While you seek him, his will
Wondering, "Is God MIA?"
Missing in action, nay"
The teacher doesn't talk
But quietly looks & stalks
As the student takes the test
Hoping to do his very best
God's waiting to do the rest.

"Wise man lay up knowledge..." (Proverbs 10:14).

C's To Transform Your Life

C-Creator. For life's purpose, direction and spirituality.
True spiritual people are like solid, strong steeples
Displaying a daily walk, talk of God's chosen people
Before, during and after sin, God provided hope, a better day
For songs, prayer and praise, he sends blessings your way
Daily seek his purpose in your life, every single moment
He speaks in your heart, your path, its' all heaven sent.

C-Communication. The key to understanding yourself and others.
A true relationship begins with communication
Listening and talking, throughout creation
Thoughts and ideas to enhance understanding
Assisting yourself and others, all withstanding
And to allow others to obtain a better understanding
Communicate with yourself, to know yourself
Communicate with others, no confusion left
Knowing how and when to communicate is crucial
Preventing wars, hatred and misunderstandings is critical.

C-Commitment. Set goals, long and short.
Goals add meaning, worth to living
Working toward a goal, sharing and giving
Each day get closer to your goal, one step make
Strive and push forth to accomplish, don't procrastinate
Enjoying what you do makes the soul at peace
Keep the faith and focus and never cease.

C-Courage of Conviction. Stand firmly on your beliefs.
Have courage, be true to something
No conviction, you'll fall for anything
Be true to whom you are, stand firm and see
Through God all things manifest to be.

C-Caring. Care for others as yourself.
Love and respect your neighbor no matter what
With kind words heal the wounded, raise those in a rut
Showing others you care, will make others care
People to people, locally, globally and everywhere
Making the difference, and joining souls
Enriching and touching, the young and old.

"Wisdom is the principal thing; therefore get wisdom: and with all thy getting get understanding." (Proverbs 4:7).

D's To Transform Your Life

D-Deliverance. To be free from bondage.
Bondage can be spiritual, physical or mental
Fear keeps you in bondage and judgmental
Free your mind and the rest of you will follow
If you don't you remain shallow, and hollow
Success comes to those who master their fear
Preventing havoc and upset to interfere
With one trying to be the best
Stopping uncertainty, insecurity, at the door rest
Faith in yourself, closes the door on fear
Believing God, to him you draw near
Acknowledge your fear, deal and proceed
Faith plus action your deliverance, plant seeds.

D-Development. Change and improvement.
Development, improvement, life is change
Many things before birth, destined, prearranged
Reaching your true potential, leap, take a step
Your mind, body and soul, you must prep
Accept, welcome and note the gains
Your entire being will begin to reign
An aging body needs physical exercises, too
An aging mind needs mental stimulation, just a few
A weary soul requires a spiritual and motivational diet
You are what you do, think and eat, so diet right.

D-Discipline. Self-control.
Discipline, self-control, as assured gateway
Mental, oral and physical powers, at your disposal lay
For the time, place and season to perform, you're there
Focused and moderated, all things clear
Allowing success, achievements to come through
Timing is the key, you will see your breakthrough.

"Say unto wisdom, Thou art my sister; and call understanding thy kinswoman:"
(Proverbs 7:4).

L's To Transform Your Life

L-Loving. Loving generates loving.
Show yourself lovable, others will return your love
Feeling loved suits the heart like a glove
Loving makes you smile and glow inside out
Love can conquer illness, and issues all about
Loving makes you talk, walk, feel alive
Requires less energy than hating, you must strive.

L-Leading. To be an effective leader, you must know how to follow.
One can not teach what one has not been taught
Leadership is learned, earned and not bought
Lead others to show them a better way
Let your leading be exemplary, don't sway
Pledge never to mislead, or misdirect
Lead by example, and often reflect.

L-Living. Live each moment of the day to its fullest.
Live this day to the utmost, regretting not a moment
Yesterday is history, focus today, well spent
Learn something new each day, big or small
Life is for progression not procrastination, make it a ball
Life has many paths, up, down and round and round
A solid decision, your destiny you're bound.

L-Leaning. Lean on the Creator for power and a sound mind.
Seek wisdom and understanding, ask God to know
The path you learn to take, you reap what you sow
Leaning on God will make you wise
Through all things, yet you rise
Lean not on your understanding
But seek to know, without grandstanding.

"The fear of the Lord is the beginning of wisdom;..." (Proverbs 9:10).

AB&C for Daily Moments

A-Accept who you are.
Know your purpose, accept who you are,
Your talent will take you near and far
It will make room for you
Open doors you never knew
Acceptance in knowing thyself
No truer purpose in life is left
Accept your potential and capabilities
Speak and believe the truth, no liability.

B-Believe in a higher power.
With meditation, prayer, a relationship with God,
Brings you closer to him, it's not a facade
Your true will is his command
But not necessarily when you demand
Believe, he only wants for you the best
All things bad, not good, he does detest
The power of life and death, reside in his hands
And he created all things throughout the lands
Believe, listen to your spirit, he guide and speaks
Superseding your intellect, by bounds and leaps
Know that all your blessings flow from him
He awaits your request, and sits at the helm.

C-Care for your fellowperson
Caring for each other would make this world a better place to live
Life is a precious gift from the Creator, to you he give
Cherish another's life as you cherish your own, you won't go wrong
Respect another's culture, always be kind
Ignore the skin color but the character you find
Each one helps one, then that one help another
Constantly caring, supporting your sister, brother.

"...to give unto them beauty for ashes, the oil of joy for mourning..." (Isaiah 61:3).

Beauty For Ashes

Exchange Beauty for Ashes, give up Godless things
Let the love of God's spirit, from within ring
Trade Beauty for Ashes, let the Unbelievers know
Fruit of the spirit, outwardly from you they flow
To the World, you're a hopeful & joyous light
Exemplifying God's grace and all things right
God's is the navigator, a guiding map
Keeping us from straying, and being a sap
With evidence of the fruit of the spirit
Outwardly they flow, your heart they sit
Love, joy, hope, peace, giving are paramount
Making life sweet, no troubles can surmount
No trials, no tribulations, no testament
Illness, worries, grief, test your percent
Of self control, fruit of the spirit in place
Determines how you soar, run and pace
All things begin and end with love
Provided you love God and seek from above
Beyond the human and physical realm
Receive Beauty For Ashes, God's at the helm
Exercise self control with mind, body and soul
Wait, keep the faith until the good times role
Life's circumstances, must be daily checked
Otherwise you may become a wreck
Self-control, a job, twenty four seven
No control, life like the seven eleven
Twenty four seven, busy, busy will abound
Much taken, your life now upside down
Be fruit of the spirit, when you don't feel good
Trade Beauty for Ashes, join God's neighborhood
As you stride, walk the walk, talk the talk
Exemplify beauty, fear not, it's God's boardwalk.

VI. LEGACY

"...Except ye be converted, and become as little children, ye shall not enter into the kingdom of heaven." (St. Matthew 18:3).

A Child Shall Lead Them

A Child Shall Lead Them, humbly each step of the way
With total reliance, and dependent on God each day
With innocence, love, trusting and caring
Following a child's play, all cares to God bearing.

A child may disagree today, tomorrow all is forgotten
Upset at this minute, happy the next, no ill-gotten
Alarmed at the answer no, forgets and moves on
Not willing to share, shares soon after, life is fun.

A Child Shall Lead Them from hatred, jealousy and distrust
A child shall teach them to disagree in love, it's a must
To be humble in understanding others, relieves strife
A child shall demonstrate appreciation, the beauty of life
And to depend one upon another, young and old
We need each other somehow, somewhere, so let's behold.

We are commissioned to love our neighbor as thyself
A Child Shall Lead Them honoring the heart, nothing else
Dissolving all wars, conflicts, to be stopped
Love in homes, communities and churches, we need to adopt.

Until we follow a child's lead there will be no peace
No harmony, no caring, no trust. We can decree
For only with humbleness, love, trust, will change
Then our life a new in God will be rearranged
Follow the example of the lad with five loaves, two fishes
Christ used to feed thousands of people full filling wishes
Let us be ready to serve our brothers and sisters locally
Let us be a keeper for our brothers and sisters, globally
If one of us stumbles and falls, we all stumble and fall
Be childlike, extend a helping hand, help another stand tall.

"I must work the works of him that sent me, while it is day: ..." (St. John 9:4).

Voices From Yesterday

Arise my child the day is yet young, don't sway
There is much work to be done, we've set the way
For you now must carry the torch this moment
Enlightening and healing, be heaven sent
Educate the young and old as you stride
Walk the walk with love at your side
Talk the talk of all things great
Making all proud and appreciate
Your stride, their living not in vain but reign.

Heed God's voice, go forth, be bold
Let wisdom, knowledge, through you unfold
Touch the hearts of others, like an eagle they soar
Then pass the torch on, others to enrich the world's core
Planting in the hearts and minds of others to seek
But never forgetting to God be meek
Asking God's Grace and mercy for today
While honoring Voices From Yesterday.

"Render therefore to all their dues; to whom tribute is due;... honour to whom honour." (Romans 13:7).

Who Do You Owe?

Every living being owes somebody, payment due
God formed you, before your parents even to you knew
Procreation through your parents, honor at best
Nurturing and caring, your caregiver did the rest
For nine months you were carried and fed
With proper nutrients, love, your daily bread
You came forth, your parents trained with footsteps to your path
Instilled morals, schooled, clothed and fed, you do the math.

Your debt was not paid just because you were born
But your life is the beginning of repayment, don't morn
A sufficient check written with your good behavior
Gratitude and obedience will suffice, let them savor.

As you mature, honor God because honor is due
Your parents for they did the best they could too
While instilling, and molding you to be
God's little precious angel, they decree.

Parents are your first teachers, mostly by example
Their traits, habits without trying you sample
With wisdom and love, they prepare the way for you.
When you stumble and fall, they lift you up, too
When your heart is broken, to it love is spoken.

Who Do You Owe? God, parents and the human race
You only have to walk in and take your rightful place
You owe many and yourself to be the best that you can be
Let your light so shine, that other might joy and see.

"And thou shalt teach them diligently unto thy children,..." (Deuteronomy 6:7).

Whose Gonna?

Children are the salt of the earth
They need to know and understand their worth
Whose Gonna educate them, if we do not?
Whose Gonna teach them leadership, if we do not?
Whose Gonna teach them the truth, our heritage
Pride, values and morals, if we do not?
Each of us should teach one and that one will teach another.

Then and only then will we begin to win the war
The war against alcohol, drugs, teenage pregnancies
Truancy, illiteracy and spiritual decadence
Then and only then can we build stronger families, communities
Churches, schools and government.

Whose Gonna continue our legacy?
If our children destroy their lives with foolishness?
Whose Gonna stand up and be a voice
If our children are incarcerated and institutionalized?
Whose Gonna teach future generations?
Whose Gonna educate, if they are unlearned?
Whose Gonna fight for our civil rights?
Whose Gonna be our future leaders, doctors, lawyers, politicians?

Your forefathers gave their lives that you may have a better life
Your history did not begin with you, but can end with you
You are just one sprung on the ladder, be a strong sprung
To support those that follow
Hatred, murders and racism, Whose Gonna fight these ills?
To eradicate them from our environment?
If you do not do your part, who will?

"Rejoice, O young man, in thy youth; and let thy heart cheer thee in the days of thy youth"… (Ecclesiastes 11:9).

Youth

Youth is but a very brief time
Changes, quick as spinning a dime
Now you have it, now you don't
Sitting and wishing, recur, it won't
Adulthood, until your dying day be
With maturity comes much responsibility
These times are here to stay
Until your very last day
Life is not a dress rehearsal, it's real
No time to fool around, nor stand still.

Drugs, alcohol, designed to destroy
Don't let anybody make you their toy
Keep yourself from these far away
Least they may destroy you some day
They affect your body, soul and mind
Making right and wrong, to you blind
Sending your life into a tail spin
And you can't remember when
Falling in love young, can make the spirit broken
Leaving you feeling like someone's used token
Don't rush your life away, your youth away
Appreciate, for it didn't come to stay.

Forsake the things that are bad
Exposure to them will make you sad
Work to do well, for it is right
Your conscience, avoid sleepless nights
A clear and healthy mind can do
A cluttered mind can only desire too
The streets of hard knocks happen for a reason
But the tunnel of hope can come in due season
Even if you make a mistake, go the wrong way
God allows U-turns anytime, any old day.

Words 'N' Action

You sit in the driver's seat
Steer clear of the wrong streets
God gave you the power
Let not drugs, alcohol, sex devour
Choose this day, the way to good
Stray from danger, all dark woods
Love your sister and brother
Give that helping hand to another
For love makes the world go round
Do it while the clock resounds
Tic toc, tic toc, tic toc, tic toc
Youth is brief, live, let it rock.

VIII. FUTURE

"Death and life are in the power of the tongue..." (Proverbs 18:21).

Destruction

The tongue a powerful tool of mass destruction
Have cultures, destroying cultures, many eruptions
Destruction and construction in the tongue lie
Like a double edge sword, can easily go off and fly
Wounding so deeply, lifetimes may not heal
In the heart anger, grief forever sealed.

The tongue is like a yin-yang
Effect all either way, a change
It can build, yet it may destroy
It can encourage, yet it may discourage
It can convey truth, yet it may lie
It can represent beauty, yet it can be ugly
It can generate, yet it may degenerate
It can support, yet it may not
It can be a peacemaker, yet it may be a peace breaker
It can be holy, yet it may be blasphemous.

From times of old, ancient and modern, throughout the lands
This powerful instrument, the tongue, many flavors, many brands
Destroying life, nature and all creation
Is faming and defaming with Nation against Nation.

In the future, for a brighter day
Let us acknowledge, speak a better way
For this power yin-yang instrument's use
It to apprehend self and others abuse.

Thou hast given him his heart's desire..." (Psalms 21:2).

Destiny

In your hands, your future, the key
Your knowledge is your decree
Future opportunities, jobs, college awaits
Choose wisely before it is too late
Countless people, paved the way for you
So open the doors, proudly walk through
Now is your turn to pave the way
Beginning, this moment, this very day
Make your parents, teachers and school proud
Let your accomplishments for you speak loud
Commitment and perseverance are your tools
Don't let nobody turn you around, make you their fool
Your life is yours to be
As great as your mind can foresee
Hold to every opportunity in sight
If you don't, another surely might.

Material things will fade
Money will disappear once made
But for you, your education is your aide
No one without your permission may invade
Will carry you to higher and higher heights
For this is your God given birthright
Many have given you the tools to succeed
Now it is up to you to take the lead
Use your inner strength and power
Let no man or woman scour
Your future, the key, lies in your hand
Hold firmly to it and take a stand
Go after what you want
And remember not to flaunt
Seek all things, for God's sake
Follow your bliss, to Destiny take

"Where there is no vision, the people perish;..." (Proverbs 29:18).

The Road To Nowhere, The Road To Somewhere

The road to somewhere begins, follow your bliss
The road to nowhere begins when you go amiss
Every human being is created for our betterment
With God's Spirit beaming through, your testament.

Eventually, everybody makes a choice and permit
But whatever the choice, you must live with it
If you strive to be something, you will be
If you aim at nothing, nothing you will see.

Doers and talkers let their energy flow
Doers do, while talkers plan to do, but never go
The doers accomplish, talkers plan to accomplish.

Choose, the road to nowhere or somewhere
Make the decision, it will take you there
Your road to go, or the road to stay
Your path is predestined, don't stray
The path you take is the path you make.

"The fear of man bringeth a snare; but whoso putteth his trust in the Lord shall be safe."
(Proverbs 29:25).

Fearfulness

Fear is a normal emotion, stirred by dread
Afraid of the unknown you make your bed
Fear, false evidence appearing real
Don't allow it to be your life's seal
Fear like electricity cause the body to short circuit
Tackle fear, eradicate with the positive, banish it
Re-channel fear, you will lead and succeed.
Fear is not to your detriment
Handling your fear, you must consent
Re-channeled fear, you are in control
Un-channeled fear, you lost you role.

Satan use fear to in bondage, you keep
With no freedom, you daily weep
God provide many ways to get away
To him you must run straightaway
If you try and stumble and fall
Fret not, just yield and heed the call
God's wants to give you true joy
Not allowing fear to you destroy.

Fear can be combated with prayer and praise
Grounding you solidly, you might be amazed
Believe in yourself, commit to God the rest
Repeat to yourself, "I can do this, fear I detest".

No one wants to fail, but failure is an option
Success is not a guarantee, but an adoption
Acknowledge your fear, then God you hear
Put on your faith, all your spiritual gear
Remove the fear mask, be about your task.

"Therefore are my loins filled with pain: pangs have taken hold upon me,..." (Isaiah 21:3).

Drowning

Life's drowning in my pain
Hurt about my body like rain
My head and heart begins to ache
Each night no sleep, I lay awake
Praying, dear Lord, please do me take
Each moment, a struggle now
Sometimes, death's better somehow
My dreams, hopes all most gone
Hard word, prayer, faith, I did sewn
Why bother, nothing seem to work
My mind, many bad thoughts lurk
All is clouded; I pray just a little sun
No where to turn, tears constantly run
Down my face, under my cheeks
The pain so deep, relief I do seek
God, where are you, I need you now
Desperately, revelation, anything somehow
A miracle, I dare say need
A mere morsel my soul to feed.

IX. CELEBRATION

"And I will bless them that bless thee,...and in thee shall all families of the earth be blessed." (Genesis 12:3).

The Gathering

A family reunion, family and friends reunite
Looking forward to greeting with much excite
Traveling joyously from near and far
Some by airplanes, trains and even by car
Reunion, a time to meet new family members
Seeing exactly who each may resemble
Greeted with the same love that now flows through
Greet them with that smile and spirit so true
Greet them with a hug, beaming like the sun
Include all in, beginning to end, fun
As you talk about the old and the new
Laugh, rejoice and refresh as long over due
Think on those who desired, but could not make it
Within your prayers, to them do not omit
Send love, a call, a card signed by all
Or pictures, recognition, no matter how small
As family, in our hearts, they were here
All will be cherish, those far and near
The old, new, and future generations are held
The love we share, give, undoubtly unparallel
For all are created out of love, each seeks love
From family, friends, and from above
Then and only then can our bonds withstand
All the fiery darts known to distract man
Destroying the family, and breaking apart
So we must seek directions and God from the start
To lead our family, friends and all humanity
Uniting in love, families uniting, a great destiny.

Words 'N' Action

Celebrate this day, food, laughter, hugs and talk
Enjoy creation, the splendor, perhaps a little walk
Love that family member, who seems unlovable
Don't forget to invite them to sit at the table
Hug that family member, who may not deserve a hug
Even though their personality personifies an old rug
Talk to that family member, who is difficult to talk to
For they too need a ear, and to talk things through
Smile at that family member, who may not deserve a smile
Stay with them long enough, a change may come after while
For with God's love all things are possible, enabled
Making lives richer, and everyone more stable
When tomorrow comes and yesterday is gone
No regrets, don't let, "I wish" be your song.

"Let the elders that rule well be counted worthy of double honour,..." (1 Timothy 5:17).

The Ones'

On this special day, at this appointed time
Let us reflect momentarily as the bell chimes
Honoring The Ones' who are no longer here
A legacy we hold in our hearts so dear
Beacons of hope, who paved the way
Surrounding us now, protecting each day
Guiding us, moment when most needed
Their new charge which God has deeded
Honor them on this day for paving the road
Ensuring our lives better, easing the load.

For knowledge, wisdom, spirituality, honor they due
Acknowledgement, appreciation, even a praise or two
Forever holding, a rich heritage, in high esteem
Never forget your history, but remain a gleam
Honor all that labored with love and admiration
On this day and henceforth, exude appreciation.

When your history, you don't know
Your are doomed to repeat as you go
Discover who you are, take the time
In the future, all will prove, genuine
Planting in your heart a sense of being
Confidence in the future will be farseeing.

"Ye are the salt of the earth:..."(St. Matthew 5:13).

The Trailblazers

Many are called, but few are chosen
Your call to duty, you have risen
Closing another chapter in God's assignment book
Joining the ranks of the past great, for many to look
Your legacy we sincerely appreciate.

Life is but mere seconds, a few gains
But if you can touch just one soul
As you pass this way
Then your living has not been in vain.

To some, you are like Esther, Queen
In spite of all odds, who remain keen
With faith, determination, no turning back
Steadfastly braved the storm to the victory track.

To others, you are like Ruth who obeyed
Through tears and disappointments, but stayed
Pursued, persevered, persisted and prayed
God open doors for which was amazed.

You may be like Deborah, upon the call of duty
Took charge of the task at hand, the persecutee
With bravery and the spirit of a warrior who rattle
Stood tall and still while God fought the battle.

Yet others may see you like Jezebel
A chosen vessel of God to thwart the rebel
Whose efforts exemplified spirituality
Seeking God's grace in life's reality.

Words 'N' Action

As you stride henceforth, God at our side
May you continually do it with dignity and pride
God deems it no other way, for he is yet in control
You will not be last, putting God first, your goal.

Your labor has generated much fruit
Some seen and some unseen will shoot
Sprouting wisdom, knowledge, love
sharing, teaching all from heavenly above.

Under the heavens, there is a purpose to all things
Purpose work, play, be, laugh even a purpose to sing
As a teacher, preacher, healer, helper or evangelist
Knowing in the name of God, there will be risk
As one member of one body with many members
Will make life bearable, no matter your gender
When one member suffers, all the members suffer
When one member rejoices, all the members rejoice
When one member is honored, all the members are honored
One cannot do without the other and should not usurp the other
But each member should compliment, and with love cement.

We salute you for your faithful and dedicated service
We salute you as you continually strive to endeavor
For being soldiers with the shield of faith
The helmet of salvation, the sword of the spirit
and the breastplate of righteousness in the army of God.

With scars on your backs, you are yet strong
Beyond all definition still defying place
Time and circumstance as you occupy space
With your strength, you are the salt of the earth
The Flavor of the Universe, the clay, our Worth.

Ask not what your church can do for you
But ask what you can do for your church.

"...and young men shall see visions, and your old men shall dream dreams:" (Acts 2:17).

Visions & Dreams

Young men have visions, it seems
While old men dream dreams
Sons of yesterday, men of today
Sons of today, men of tomorrow
To the elder man, accomplishments you deed
To the younger man, watch and take heed.

Brothers today is a new day, unlike yesterday
Yesterday's strategies are obsolete
The human race needs workers who can't be beat
Not old men talking of what they have done
Young men watching like baring a ton
And a few saying can't we all get along.

Elder men teach the young, their history, to reverence God
Exemplify courage, love, strength, respect, as they plod
To honor the sisters, mothers, cherish the children
for life is too short not to share a smile or grin
Be a parent to the fatherless, a brother to the brotherless
Be a friend, to he who has no friend
Listen to the young, you may learn too
Hug your son, your brother, a touch goes a long way
Positive images breed positive examples, forever stay.

Work while it is day, when night comes no man can work
Be sober in your doings, thinking, let no one control your thoughts
Least you may be mislead, misused and miss-educated
These ills, a life must not be built and predicated.

Words 'N' Action

"Now also when I am old and grayheaded, O God, forsake me not:..." (Psalm 71:18).

Forerunners

Seniors this is your day, high regards your way
Appreciatively, we honor and acknowledge you
For all you have done, doing and about too
For the hearts you have touched, am touching
The smiles you have shared and yet sharing
Your life's impact, made many joyously react
Your life represents jewels more precious than any stone
Your sharing and giving was given freely, not on loan
Freely given and freely received, too thee
Tangibles and intangibles you shared with glee.

Your footsteps are deeply planted everywhere you trod
Your footsteps leave a path to be followed like a rod
Your footsteps have their place in history and time
Your footsteps shall guide the future generations down the line
Your footsteps have made us proud of you on this special day
And you should be proud of yourself and delight in every way.

Be proud in who you are, who God has made you
Be proud in your accomplishments, they are true
Be proud in your wisdom and knowledge, for we are
Be proud in the example you exemplify, passing many by far
Be proud and others will be proud with you, your light be right.

Seniors you are like trees and branches
All together a powerful and strong avalanche
Leaders of yesterday, a solid world tomorrow we see
Your nourishment for the younger, we thankfully decree
Your longevity, good health, a sound mind
Be proud of your years, nature has been kind
Longevity has its victories and defeats, take a seat
As you recite, no victories, no testimony, no defeats
No maturity, no wisdom gained, to sustain
We proudly salute you, for being you, true grain.

"...to the which also ye are called in one body; and be ye thankful." (Colossians 3:15).

Thanksgiving

On this special day, give thanks to the Creator for life and blessings
If we say we love the Creator whom we have not seen
What about that brother, sister, mother, father, or child whom we have seen
Who oftentimes tugs at our heart strings beyond believability.

Be thankful for your family, not only because God ordained it
But because we all need love, caring and belonging
Even dysfunctional families have benefits
Better an imperfect family, than no family at all
For there are not any perfect families
The grass always looks greener on the other side.

Take time to say thanks to that Mother you took for granted
That Father who did the best he could and was there
Thank them for what they did and forget what they did not do
Show your gratitude, better late than never.

Be thankful for that child who excels
Be thankful for that child who does not
For the apple does not fall to far from the tree
This is your little apple, round and red or oblong and green.

Thank that mentor who struggled with you through the bad and the good
Who was your backbone when you were to weak to stand
Whose belief in you lit the path to a brighter road
Take a moment and say, "I am because of you, thank you."

Be thankful for that job, however a drudgery
The jobless wish they had a job
Be thankful for that home, unlike your neighbor's
The homeless have no home
Be thankful for that car, no longer being manufactured
For many are without and wish they had.

Words 'N' Action

Everyday you awake, that day is the first day of the rest of your life
Live it to the fullest, enjoy the fragrance of life to the fullest
Take in the freshness of each new day, inhale life and exhale thanks.

Life is a journey, some journeys are short, others long
As you journey through this life, pick the roses
Smell the lilies, enjoy the sun, take a deep breath
And thank the Creator with all your heart and soul.

"Every man shall give as he is able..." (Deuteronomy 16:17).

Accommodation

Best wishes exudes from this phonograph
For kind deeds, sharing on all behalf
Accept this token of thanks, appreciation
For making a difference, throughout creation
Reflecting on days, weeks, months and year
Knowing your efforts, to my eyes come a tear
For all the joy and love throughout you bring
Makes the heart with admiration sing
For all the good, the people you do
Changing lives, through and through
You serve with a quality well admired
Never showing one, you are too tired
To listen, to heed, to chat and smile
Making hearts wanting to stay awhile
Unto you is given, while you have eyes to see
And know, you are sweeter than honey bee
While words may fade away, memories linger on
With joy in your heart, pray you carry on
Making a difference each and every day
In your own unique and very special way
Your reward lies before, and within you
As you share your soul, through and through.

"But the fruit of the Spirit is love, joy, peace..." (Galatians 5:22).

Acquaintanceship

During Acquaintanceship, many lives intersect
Hearts are opened and embraced like a net
Doing everything possibly that one could
With warm hospitality, like only one would
Today, let us acknowledge this special day
Your love spewed out, in every which way
For this makes you many things to many people
Standing tall like a giant glowing steeple
Within creation, you are a mentor of glee
With eyes of wisdom, all things you see
Loving & caring, affecting as if leaven
Making the difference, just like heaven.

To honor, cherish, celebrate, proudly, we salute you
With all the beauty, honor and love, that you're due
For being graceful and spiritual through & through
And second to none, fresher and fresher, never blue
Being one of God's astounding mature creation
Aligning in perfect harmony, God's purpose formation
Children, adults, young and old, and friends too
Testifies to all your efforts, you had a lot to do
Much appreciation and many stories to share and tell
Their love, admiration and adoration rings like a bell.

A leader, a guide, an educator, a few attributes
How you did it, persevered, no one can compute
Being the first, a champion of causes, I say
Knocking down doors, opening the way
Good news, Heaven must be missing an angel
On earth, you rule and reign, yet never strangle
Now resides in the midst of much care and love
Flapping your wings like a beautiful brilliant dove
Winning souls for Christ, no matter how long
With words, wisdom and maybe even a song.

Words 'N' Action

Admiration, jubilation, all that you have earned
In the midst of all, you weathered and sojourned
Each smiles, reflect on all you've gave and done
Just know each step of the way, a title well earned.

Through trials and tribulations you stood fast
Accomplished a lot, memories will forever last
A champion, you are the trooper of the hour
We honor you for being, and never sour
With a heart and spirit so big
We are proud to be a part of this shin dig
Saluting a great and deserving humanitarian, I know
And won't think twice to tell you so
As we give flowers of love, and dare say
From warm hearts comes, "This Is Your Day"!

"Deck thyself now with majesty and excellency; and array thyself with glory and beauty."(Job 40:10).

A Majesty For All Seasons

Today these words comes your way
To allow my heart, and thoughts to convey
My genuine appreciation for having known
All your efforts and care that you've shown
People like you, your deed, I gratefully behold
Excitingly thanking God, while others are told
Of your generosity throughout all seasons
Gives me joy, and a most profound reason
To pray that God shines blessings upon you
Success, good health and wealth too
Making your journey in life
As good as can be, and less strife
For your humanitarian deeds, you're the best
Sets you apart, and above the rest
When I think on you, on my face a smile
My heart leaps and jumps at least a mile
With gladness, thanks and joy
You make the difference, and I say
Each and everyday, in a lovely & kind way
Truly a majesty for all seasons
Your life bespeaks, I reason.

Words 'N' Action

"I have fought a good fight, I have finished my course,..." (II Timothy 4:7).

Warriors

Man's worth determined by his sacrifices, how he live
Many are better off for you, since you voluntarily give
The greatest reward doing for others and having done so
When duty called, you arouse, never thought the word no
Because of you, safety and security, Christmas comes everyday
With you risking and fighting the Iraq war, I proudly dare say
In spite of danger, you remain at war, and fight
Allowing us to live in peace, our Country's plight
Bombs, traps, gun firing and danger all around
You stand tall and challenge, no complaint or sound
Away from home and love ones, we appreciate
Your ultimate sacrifice for us, it is first rate
We wait with open arms and love at the gate
My thoughts sometimes filled with pain
Knowing bullets, bombs around you rain
Yet as a National, you're steadfast and remain
So when I pray, know your efforts are not in vain
Each time I think on you, I call to God your name
That you find peace in your state, just the same
Prayers that God will protect, comfort and keep
And no danger or disasters, in Iraq you reap
We await your safe return home, to family and friends
With much honor and appreciation, a new life begins
Being at War on Christmas day, know you are dearly missed so
By all your fellow Countrymen & Women, this you should know
Keep in mind as time goes on, the War, one day soon will pass
As we see the atrocities, I pray that this War will truly be our last
Appreciation in our History books, notes a job well done
Your legacy ingrained in history, your duty no one can shun
Fighting a war, the ultimate sacrifice, you deserve the best
Upon your return with love, joy, and honor you rest
As I think on Men and women like you, I admire
Sending you Christmas greetings and prayers, I never tire
Until you're safely home again with joy

Words 'N' Action

Singing your praises, I won't be coy
Heroes and She-roes are not born but made
Your commitment, memories shall never fade
Without you, this Country has no peace
Because of you, Iraq's devastation will cease
Giving Iraqi's boys and girls a chance
To be free and honor you at a glance
Because of you, fewer lives in fear
Knowing happiness & joy is so near
Because of you, many can smile
Thoughts of your efforts, stretch a mile
Know that your presence, the ultimate testament
During the war, we send our highest sentiments!

"He that tilleth his land shall be satisfied with bread..." (Proverbs 12:11).

Faithful Ambassador

Yesterday is gone, tomorrow is uncertain, today is here
For your great Godly deeds we honor you with cheer
Unwavering service, with laughter and tears
For faithful service, throughout the years.

With your sharing, you went that extra step
And wisdom guided you from right to left
With your love, all was made to feel at home
Spiritually and naturally, not one was left alone
Freely you gave, the goodness of God, complete
A little love goes a long way, sometimes repeat
With your inspiration, you inspire the uninspired
With your gentleness, you lifted the downtrodden
You reached the un-reached, your way
Encourage the discouraged, without delay.

As you stride toward God's pyramid for your life
Your niche found you, piercing others like a knife
Knowing your path, you stride full forth
With pleasure and enjoyment, about your girth
For you saw the light at the other end of the tunnel
Walked toward the light, as your joy was funnel
Being an example, when God lead, God keeps
His Grace was sufficient and you did reap
Do unto others, as you will have them do unto to you
Be assured, that God is proud, through and through.

"...to be absent from the body, and to be present with the Lord." (II Corinthians 5:8).

Commemoration

Beautiful flowers are created by God
For his pleasure, and ours he nod
On this occasion, we celebrate a rose
A Dear, loved so much, as the story goes
Who made a difference, while traveling this way
bringing joy, love, hope and a smile to our way
Truly love is a many splendor things
Thinking upon makes the heart sings
The warmth, smile and touch brought all joy
While loving others completely, and never coy
Work was a joy every step and each day
Preparing the best for all, a special way
The void left will never ever be the same
The memory and love will infinitely remain
While the spirit towers completely about the room
With brilliance ambiance, glowing like a moon
A persona of strength and character was great to behold
Always greeting with a warmth, gentleness, yet bold
Took much pride and love, but never sway
Given so much, many times, got carried away
Enjoying the moment, filled with love
Exuding from within, like a floating dove
with a melody like soft jazz emitting, what a delight
Making every encounter so wonderful and just right
This Life's ship was ran with poignancies, pride and tight
Never recorded as second to none, a Dear, out a sight
With all that was done to make another heart glad
Missing this beauty and touch, makes us very sad
God gave this joy to us, now we must return it to God
"Tis better to have loved and lost than never to have loved at all!"

"Delight thyself also in the Lord; and he shall give thee the desires of thine heart." (Psalm 37:4).

Lasting Impression

Lasting impression, so many you have made
You opened your heart, embraced, and gave
Doing everything possibly that you could
Ensuring love in the air, like only you would
In return we champion you, this very day
Giving back the love, you've shown in every way
You are many things to many people
Standing tall like a giant steeple
I hear, full of Godly wit & wisdom too
Sharing all around, through and through
Relentless giving much to many lives
Bring joy, even shooting the jive
Loving to share, your portions are big
Fruitfulness, weighing tons, like a rig
Some say you're a loyal, a trusted friend
Standing by to help, assist to the very end
You shop for others, one of many claims to fame
Oh my, you buy in dozen, with or without a name
Affording your bosom to swell and overflow
Gifts to fit all or any, from head to toe
You possess a great eye for very beautiful things
Clothes, shoes, handbags, jewelry, that sings
Driving is an art form, behind the wheel, you pack
While running errands, making all others step back
Never skip a beat, with energy to spare
To encourage, support, love, and share
You have a heart full of gold
Many have seen, others told
A personality, delightful and ole so sweet
Doing many kind deed, as you amazingly entreat
You extend a helping hand to one and all
As you hear the cry, you answer the call
Steadfastly, you've remained the same
Down to earth, and too boot, you got game.

"Every man shall give as he is able,..." (Deuteronomy 16:17).

The Veteran

Years of service, a thing of the past, the old
With memories, stories and fun to behold
To have known was too adore him
Soft spokeness, smiles, nothing can dim
In our hearts, remains the wit and love
And gentleness, forever soft like a dove
Remembering the heartfelt jokes often told
Brings laugher even now to the young and the old
Referred to by comrades and others, the Brother
Revered and greeted, as the man like no other
Gentle, friendly and easy going
Left everyone affected and glowing
Had many siblings, the youngest boy
Yet gentle, and special, and even coy
At the ripe and tender age of fourteen
Had a vision and a dream to be seen
Then upped his age by a notch or two
Off to the US Army, hurriedly flew
Defending his Country, with an upped age
To the United States Army, became engaged
Boot camp to Duty, the marriage began
With armor, to his assignment he ran
Seeking to see the many wonders of the world
Venturing, place to place, as a solider he twirled
For many, many years traveling the skies
Defending, helping, assisting many lives
A man of valor and determination
Gave his heart and soul to Our Nation
Fighting Korean, World War II and Vietnam
Leaving no regrets, and nothing to be scam
Determined to make a difference, yet wounded
Using his God given talent, many he astounded
Two purple hearts, a bronze star, just the same
Recognition, awards, ribbons, much honor came

Words 'N' Action

Being a Private with joy, rose to the top
With bravery and dedication, nothing to stop
All this done, many years, then retired
Returning, soul now rest, greatly admired
Among family & friends, now enjoys life
To the fullest, while avoiding all strife
Wisdom expounded, often over dinner
Teaching all, pursue, be a winner
Known from a child, being loyal and kind
Even in absence, remained on one's mind
Left by a smile, burned so deeply in a spot
Like a fire flamed, now simmering so hot
To many he was son, brother, uncle, husband, dad
All agree, loyalty, soft spoken, kindness was his tag
To be in that presence, what a charm
To have been, yet rings like an alarm
This life's legacy shall daily attest
An altruist to the world, was the best
A passioned journey makes life worth living
Affecting like a love song, eternally singing.

"Marriage is honourable in all, and the bed undefiled:..." (Hebrews 13:4).

The Union

One day God created male and female
Man, fairly easy, female a hard sale
Nevertheless, our first family to date
Generations, to generations, soon to placate
Sprouting everywhere all sorts of little people
Traveling the earth, towering like steeples
God created the family to honor and love
Bonding together like his prairie doves
Making music and to God they sing
Love and adoration, their voices ring.

There once was a lady who patiently waited
Who met many men and contently abated
One day a special man would appear
Glowing and smiling with love so dear
Her heart was touched, with much delight
He smiled and spoke, she knew he was right
For matrimony, he eagerly extended his hand
Into his comforting arms, she hurriedly ran
Setting a date, the two did soon wed
Living in bliss, off they led
To see the love within their eyes
Yes God ordained, for they are wise
Watching them as they work together
Bringing sunshine to all types of weather
Reaching out to others, their claim to fame
Love, Joy and peace, should be their name
Money, food, home, they give to all
Without hesitation, no thought overall
God created male and for him to forbear
With woman assist, he goes everywhere
This loving, blessed couple, walk the walk
As God light their path to talk the talk
Wisdom, knowledge, a badge of honor
Many are the recipient of these two donors

To behold the beauty, the two of them share
Makes one glad, just knowing they care
When special people, enter into your life
Enjoy the love and giving, avoiding strife
Give each other flowers long overdue
Celebrate with love, through and through
Those that God has joined together
Are unique and special, as they stir
Making footsteps for all humankind to follow
Making the world a lot better and not hollow
Urging all to pursue, commend the best
Find your purpose, stand tall above the rest
To have missed their love, a deadly sin
Receiving then, assuredly you win
You make the difference, we love you so
Our hearts leap with joy, as the story go
Know that you make the difference on Earth
These words ring out, to celebrate your worth
Blessings to you, for many kind deeds
All will return to you, as you plant and seed
To give love and help is to gain
Many thank you, shower like rain
May God bless you, at your best do
Love each other, unite many, God unto.

"…and to be a joyful mother of children. Praise ye the Lord." (Psalm 113:9).

Mother, A Rose

A rose is still a rose
Through the storms and the rain
A rose is still a rose
Any day or any hour
No matter what, a rose will be a rose
Sharing beauty with all that beholds.

Mother, your are A Rose
Over the years you have proven to stand tall
Sharing love, joy and understanding with all
You never wavered in your authenticity
You always remained the rose you are.

You are my refreshing, and charming rose
When I had crosses to bear, you were there
Made me stronger during my weaker moments
Shared wisdom when guidance was needed
Wiped my tears with love and understanding
Laugh with me during my triumphs
Encouraged me to pursue my dreams
To reach not only for the sky but the stars, alike
To run the race, and don't get weary
For in due time, God will provide
You supported all my endeavors
Cheering me on as if I was running a marathon
You were my head cheerleader of the hour
A cheerleader that an athletic can only dream of
"It is not where you are springing from
But where you are springing too."

Words 'N' Action

My Rose, thank you for giving me life, love and nurturing
And more importantly over the years yourself
God could not have given me a better role model
I am thankful for your beauty that glows from within, without
Providing unconditional love & beauty like only a rose could.

Today, everyday, salutations are to you do, My Rose
For being special in your words, touch and smile
A very special lady that is great to behold
By the young and the old
Because you bring laughter, joy and love to us all
Many lives are more enrich, like a rose, you stood tall
The Words, "If I can just touch one life as I travel
This way then my living has not been in vain"
My Rose, rest assured your living is not in vain
Your loving touch will defy time, place and circumstances
May your beauty forever entrance those you behold
And those that behold you, alike, today henceforth.

Words 'N' Action

"Train up a child in the way he should go:..." (Proverbs 22:6).

Father, A Root

A Root is grounded in the earth
Allowing no other to takes its' turf
Firmly planted and unmovable
Created by God, to lead and enable
Your family to flourish
While you work to nourish
With all your daily efforts
Fulfilling God's forte
The home, family with all your love
Ensuring needs are met, fit like a glove
You were the first in God's creation
You are the first, in family formation
God gave you wife, a help meet
Assisting you in every little beat
Together you populate the earth
With little ones about your girth
Crying and seeking, you diligently heed
Fulfilling all my childish needs
When I cried, the very beginning
You were there cheering & grinning
As a father you have always tried
Important request, I was never denied
As a father, you was always there
Allowing me to know that you truly care
And wanted me to be the best
Stand tall, be proud and in God we rest
You set the example, to be followed
Even when I appeared to be shallow and hollow
Your love daily, around me surround
Making me strong, solid and sound
You led me each step of life's way
While you kept danger at bay
When I needed a strong hand you were there
When I needed a gentle touch, love was in the air

Words 'N' Action

You my root, I honoring you for whom you are
Superseding so many others by far
Now on your very special day, Father's Day
I am proud and honored in every way
To send my love, thanks and appreciation
You're my hero, my total inspiration!

XII. AVOCATION

"Let another man praise thee, and not thine own mouth;..." (Proverbs 27:2).

The Praiser

Always seek to praise another
Even if it's not your brother
Accept criticism to construct
Reject criticism you self destruct
Mopping and potting, bad response
Sometimes making you feel like a dunce
Insecurity with job, family and self
Your heart open, displayed on a shelf
Any criticism fuel on the amber feeds
Burning you internally, totally like a weed
Perfectionism, a trait your self enslaved
Defecting growth, an early grave
Much criticism, every fiber upset
Forcing you to repel like a super jet
Even though you did you very best
Sometimes unnoticed, and laid at rest
Work, labor, not your personhood
But just the medium, for your good
Jesus was often and many criticized
Because of him, I rise, and still I rise
God chastise for your betterment
Transforming you into quite a mint
Parents comment to make you strong
Helping you to avoid some wrong
Life is always about living and learning
Why not take heed and enjoy the journey.

"Mine eyes are ever toward the Lord;..." (Psalm 25:15).

One Race, One Prize

Humans are the one true race
Honor due to one God, our prize
Each has a journey to fulfill
All in line with God's will
You are destined to do and be
Go within yourself to see
God's reason, your presence here
Make things better, don't you fear
All your tools created within
Pursue your dream, you will win
A lawyer, doctor, teacher or judge
Admire others but don't begrudge
There's only one true race
We're altogether, go at your pace
Be sure, keep your eye on the prize
Blessings to come befitting your size
What's your's, cannot be taken
Soar like an eagle, don't be mistaken
Life awaits, humanity to be better
Be positive and weather the weather
The cloud, the storm now moving on
Leaving you a bit higher on the rung
Run the race, keep your pace
Evil alerts, God's your mace
Giving your sheer delight
While passing through, you see the light.

"...If ye continue in my word, then are ye my disciples indeed;..." (St. John 8:31).

The Called

God hasn't called you to just work
Struggling and barely surviving the dirt
He has mainly called you to win
Be thankful & proud to the very end
When that friend, turns their back
Approach with love, and not attack
When that job, no longer there
God's got a lamb in the bush somewhere
When mother and father are gone
Remember, God can't do no wrong
Those that are called by his name
No matter what, will triumph just the same
If you are one of the chosen called
Don't you worry, just be, stand tall
To be called, an honor bestowed by God
Load his word, on your new ipod
In the end, it's all your's to win
Just don't give in, yourself to sin
That blocks God's channel through you flow
Missing blessings after blessings as you go
Know that only the strong survive
Provided you've got God on your side
The called are the leaders of the day
Showing others the road to freedom way
Be like the lilies of the field, birds in the air
Knowing God is there with love to spare
Be thankful for being the called
Set apart, Godlike, most of all.

"Give, and it shall be given unto you; good measure, pressed down, and shaken together..." (St. Luke 6:38).

The Giver

We feel we have all the answer
So smart, we can't eradicate cancer
Yes, there are many things one can do
Only because God has allowed one too
We feel we have all control
Yet death shakes and confirms our role
There is a power greater and beyond
Go within find God and seek to bond
Let God be God, direct your path
So many chances, you do the math
Miraculously astounding you'll be
A better life, watch, you're see
Let God be God, many rewards abound
Effortlessly, about you and all around
The more you honor, the greater your seed
Give to another, meet your neighbors need
Don't overlook nor forget not the needy
Receive from others but don't be greedy
Positive energy, a smile makes
Someone's day, and joy awakes
Let God be God beaming through
Like sunlight on the mountain dew
Making a difference in the world we live
Through your life, to others you give.

"I waited patiently for the Lord, and he inclined unto me, and heard my cry." (Psalm 40:1).

Don't Count Me Out

When you're low, look high, you're find me
Waiting with two gloves to box life with
I light the way, you stomp the way
Within thee, I lie and wait
All you have to do is seek
Earnestly seek, a tear, gentle cry, prayer
Even a tiny little whisper, gets my attention
I'm just waiting, you want all that is good
I want all that is the best for you
I will send a teacher, preacher, stranger
Even a child I send, to heal your pain,
Illuminate your path, soothe your aching heart
Dry up your tears, fulfill your dreams
Exhale your loneliness, breathe in comfort
Even while low, give you tools to help another
Seed, time and harvest, my grace is sufficient
It doesn't matter what you're going through
My arms await to gently pull you through
Leap, I'm waiting to catch you
As you fly, I hold you up as you soar like an eagle
High above you fly, landing like a champion
Like Joseph, from the dungeon to the Palace
Like Ruth, from rags to riches
Like Paul, from torment to peace
Like Eve, from shame to forgiveness
Like Thomas, from doubt to belief
Like Peter, with faith walking on water
Like birds, bees, trees, animals, I clothe them too
Whatever state you find yourself in be content
And know that I am yet God and has no respect of person
Black, brown, white, red, I created all, to be childlike
If you have a need, don't fret, try me and be free
Don't Count Me Out, I'm on the case, with Grace, this race.

"...walking in the midst of the fire, and they have no hurt;..." (Daniel 3:24).

The Fiery Furnace

Each life is unique and contained
Some days it pours mountains of rain
Some days the sun shines all so bright
With all you touch, being so right
When days are barren, dreary, and dark
Your back feels broken, you're stuck in park
Trying to drive forward, sadness pulls you back
You're in the Fiery Furnace, God's got your back
Like Shadrach, Meshach, & Abednego was under attack
They stood in the fire, and not a scorch or burn
God stepped in, protected each way they turn
They stood their faith, it showed them the way
Life was bleak and barren, this unique day
But when tomorrow arose, their statue was high
For God fought their battle, without a sigh
Stand in the fiery finance, and know it can't burn
As long as you know God and wait your turn
The fire will smoldered, the smoke will cease
For this too shall pass, onto another season
Just note you're the better, from this you reason
The Fiery Furnace maybe all you've got
But know with God's help, it ain't so hot.

"...Greet ye one another with an holy kiss." (1 Corinthians 16:20).

The Greeting Kiss

Greet that family member, with a kiss, like a true friend
That true friend, with a kiss, like a family member to the end
That stranger, like a friend or family member
Even when their ways, morals, don't resemble
Greet each other with respect and love from above.

Welcome that stranger like you desire to be welcomed
for that stranger may become your best friend or confidant
for that stranger may be there to pick you up when you are down
for that stranger may become closer than a brother or sister and stick around
for that stranger may become your husband, wife or in-law
Family and friends bond everyday, until your last
Allowing no ills to destroy, but commit to the past
Be a teacher, a trainer, to all who needs
Even unto the stranger, do a good deed
Do not allow ignorance to destroy
We are all one, one soul, by far
Our spirituality, allow us to cease
Violence against another, no but peace
Unwed mothers, fathers, drugs and thievery, strange indeed
Sometimes causing havoc around, spreading like weeds
A friend, a stranger, a family member, their creed
Entertain the heart, and not destroy the pedigree.

This is indeed the day that the Creator has made
Let us be glad, rejoice in it and make the grade
Rejoice for the good, the bad, and to everyone give
Make the World, tomorrow a better place to live
Family, friends, strangers and all
Commission yourselves together, be enthralled
Each one teach one, each one reach one
Each one love one, that one will be a clone.

XII. AMERICAN HISTORY

" I have been sick, and I have been tired, now I am sick and tired of being sick and tired and these no teaching teachers and chicken eating preachers." Mrs. Hamer

Mrs. Fannie Lou Hamer, The Majorette

A hero becomes some, some become a hero
Making a difference, aside putting their ego
Life's struggles, issues so many were forced
To pursue, eradicate, many others coerced
There was no back seat in Mrs. Fannie Lou Hamer,
Confronting all, a manner, no one would blame her
With determination, her destiny to fulfill
Being unstoppable, even when feeling ill
Twelve sisters and brothers, her family had
With little education, she was a curious lad
Noting the difference between Black and White
Her spirit knew, this couldn't be right
Going to church was barren, just routine
Sunday after Sunday, no changes to be seen
William Chapel was beginning to attest
Martin Luther King, our determination rest
Perry Hamer, her husband, backbone and tower
Never wavering, stood still, every devoted hour
All good privileges, appeared out of sight
But she was determined to make things right
Being sick and tired of being sick and tired
Changing the System, proved no easy ride
The Winona jail beatings, humanly horrific, bad
Standing for equal rights, made the police mad
Mrs. Hamer took abuse, suffered beatings long enough
But life before Civil Rights struggles was also rough
She was beaten for no apparent reason
As if she had committed a crime, treason
She suffered a lot, but proudly stood still
Not letting no one break her stride, her will
Marchings, lynchings, bus rides did not deter
With faith, fight, support, Ruleville got better
Joining SCLC, to bring about a better change

Words 'N' Action

The more she did, the more she got a name
Voting rights, equal rights, she fought to pass
Determined these denials would not last
Beatings and jailings, her course she remain
Determined to tell the world, Mississippi's game
People being denied rights to vote and just live
Always the Negro denied and had to give
With determination, she went from the cotton fields
To the Halls of Congress to eradicate the ills
Born into family of sharecroppers, seeking a better way
Hard work, no rights, forced her to stand one great day
She stood this day, determined she had something to say
June Johnson, Ivesta Simpson, Lawrence Guyot, Annelle Ponder
And Ms. Hamer suffered atrocities, unveiled publicly like thunder
The National Democratic Convention, she truthfully spoke
The World was alarmed, on the details nearly choked
People in the southern town, a better life so held back
By chicken eating preachers, no teaching teachers who lacked
She ran for office of State Senate
Didn't win, Charles McLaurin go in it
Freedom Farm was dear to her heart
Feeding the hungry from the upstart
MFDP fought a strong, courageous fight
Identifying wrongs, to make them right
Many fought and died, names untold
Just like our forefathers, transported and sold
Medgar Evers, James Chaney, Michael Swerner, Andrew Goodman
Gave their lives, fought tirelessly, in spite of the Ku Klux Klan's men
 NJ, Washington, Chicago, MFDP convention she attended
Just to be seated required much effort, much amendment
Credentials committee, the President, Hoover, had to see
We was determined not to let things remain and be
Some enslaved, while others are free
Not the way, God intended to be
FBI and Justice Department, did a lot to stop
But she was determined to reach the top
Being seated at the convention, sent many for a swirl
We're here, "America is home, like the rest of the world."

"Every man must decide whether he will walk in the light of true altruism or in the darkness of destructive selfishness." Martin Luther King Jr.

Dr. Martin Luther King, Jr., The Drum Major

There are many beautiful flowers in the Garden of God
Today, we shall water one of these beautiful flowers, that has reached immortality
Dr. Martin Luther King Jr., for his deeply rooted humane efforts
And his commitment to God's purpose for all mankind
Dr. King fought a good fight, ran a difficult race
Incarceration in the Birmingham County Jail, did not break his stride
The March from Selma to Montgomery, did not break his stride
Bombings, shootings, murders, unfair court rulings, did not break his stride
In Memphis, Tennessee, an evil force took his mortal body but not his soul
For he had been to the mountaintop, his eyes had seen the coming of the Lord.

Today, as he rest in the spiritual realm, we honor him for his living was not in vain
We celebrate him for his noble sense of purpose, strength to withstand
The jeering faces of hostile mobs, agonizing loneliness, jim crowism
And peer pressure even while sitting in a Birmingham jail cell
With tired feet, a great sense of humor, and his soul at rest
He persevered through the seen and unforeseen like a Drum Major
He lead the parade of non-violent freedom fighters
He advocated, that Freedom would never be voluntarily given up by the oppressor
But must be demanded by the oppressed
That segregation is a disease, and festers at the roots of America's Soul
That justice too long delayed is justice denied
That there is no justice, while your first name is nigger, and your middle Name is boy, and your last name is John
That this Country cannot survive half free and half slave
That injustice anywhere is a threat to justice everywhere
Over four hundred years in America, the African Americans are still not free
Life is yet crippled by chains of segregation, racism and discrimination
In this land of plenty, we are yet forced to reside on poverty islands
And made to feel America, is not really our home

America is yet giving us a bad check, stamped with insufficient funds
America's bank of justice is nowhere near bankrupt
In the great vaults of opportunity, this Nation owe us a long overdue refund
Politically, educationally, and economically
Let us honor Dr. King's legacy by continually striving for freedom
But do not drink of the cup of bitterness and hatred but love and peace
Maybe someday we can rise up and live as God intended
Maybe then children of former slaves and children of former slaves owners
Can live together and be judged by the content of their character
And not by the color of their skin. Free at last, than God Almighty, Free at last!

"Many whites, even white Southerners, told me that even though it ma have seemed like the Blacks were being freed, they felt more free and at ease themselves. They thought that my action didn't just free Blacks but them also." Mrs. Rosa Parks

Mrs. Rosa Parks, The Innovator

Mrs. Parks, a strong, courageous woman who wore many hats
A seamstress, modern day civil rights mother, advocate at bat
She refused a bus driver request; give up her seat, for a White
Tired and weary, this day no such luck, this can't be right
He was the same bus driver, who had evicted her years before
The year of 1943, this first time, she rose and exit the bus door
But years later, December 1, 1955, her refusal led to her arrest
Montgomery forever changed, hundreds, and thousands protest
The Country's unrest, 381days long Montgomery Bus Boycott
Claiming her seat, proclaiming her rights, everything got might hot
This successful boycott, for which Dr. Martin Luther King Jr. led
Was won through taunts, physical abuse, and much blood shed
Commitment was the motto, seeking and looking any day for change
Northern whites join the Blacks, some Southerners became deranged
Often time threats ensued to run the Northerners from whence they came
Murders, lynchings, they stood their ground, sided with, just the same
All this came about, Mrs. Parks's dignity, courage, and pride
Determined this day, with tired feet, she would ride
Mrs. Parks, an ever-present quiet strength to the end
Remained committed making the crooked straight, not bend
Being fired from her tailoring job, she changed her way
Physically moving, but mentally from politics never strayed
Off to Detroit, a better life to be had, she moved
Nothing broke her stride, continued her groove
Detroit and other battle grounds, she remained
An activist for twenty five years, she did reign
Now she reside in the heavens around, and above
Seeking to guide, assist, as she hovers like a dove
A lady's work is never done, always reflecting like the sun.

"Life shrinks or expands in direct proportion to the courage with which we live it."

Mrs. Victoria Adams, A True Champion

As a Teacher, Mother, Businesswoman, Wife, she was first rate
She traveled the World, inspiring, leaving her mark on the gate
She served in capacities, titles, to many to name and count
Check out her path, many accomplishments will surmount
Churches, schools, political organizations, were her second home
She laid foundations, a legacy for many to travel and roam
Seven decades of contributions to society, the World, she gave
Honored with awards, citations, appreciations, many raved
Newspapers, films, documentaries, books, posters, she is graced
For she fought a good fight, stayed her course, ran and raced
Being a native of Mississippi, injustices caused her to act
Destroying society's hills, racism, seeking a better track
Victoria Adams, a towering figure passed this way
Therefore we must champion her efforts, without delay
For all the inroads, strides, foundations she laid
Ensuring a better life for all civil rights she made
First Black, Mississippi woman, United States Senate she ran
Along with Mrs. Hamer, Senate seated, a first in this land
Death threats, violence, murders, beatings, she never refrain
Knowing what she must do, determined, steadfastly remain
SNCC, SCLC, MFDP attest to her unwavering spirit to be
For all the hard work, struggles, a better day all would see
Seeking voting privileges, ending segregations was a goal
Allowing all to be treated fairly, justly, human as a whole
She taught voter registration, literacy classes, encouraged all
To fight for freedom and civil rights, educate, and stand tall
Today we champion her, for the footsteps that she has laid
Let's us never forget, but teach others, the life price she paid.

"Ye are the salt of the earth:…" (St. Matthew 5:13).

The Flavor Of The Universe

Many are chosen, but few are called
You have been called to duty on this occasion
As you close another chapter in God's assignment book
May you join the ranks of the greatest who precedes you
May you leave a legacy for those that proceed after you.

Life is but mere seconds
But if you can touch just one soul as you pass this way
Then your living has not been in vain.

To some, you are like Esther
In spite of all odds against you
With faith and determination
You were steadfast and braved the storm to victory.

To others, you are like Ruth
Through tears and disappointments
You pursued, persevered and persisted
And God showed you a better way.

You may be like Deborah, upon the call of duty
You took charge of the task at hand
With bravery and the spirit of a warrior
You stood tall and still while God fought your battle.

Yet others may see you like Sojourner Truth, Harriet Tubman
Mahalia Jackson, Ida B. Wells, Fannie Lou Hamer
Mary McCleod Bethune, Madame C.J. Walker, Phyllis Wheatley
Marian Anderson, Rosa Parks, Maya Angelou, Mother Hale
But more importantly, you are seen as a chosen vessel of God
Your work exemplifies your spirituality
Your talk dictates God's grace
Your walk confirms that you are indeed one of God's ambassadors
As you stride henceforth

May you continually do it with pride and dignity
God deems it no other way, for he is yet in control
Put God first and you will not be last
Your labor has generated much fruit
Some seen and some unseen
Fruits of wisdom, knowledge, love
Sharing, teaching and role modeling
Under the heavens there is a time to every purpose
And a purpose for every time and every work
You may be teacher, preacher, healer, helper or evangelist
Whatever, you are but one member of one body with many members
When one member suffers, all the members suffer
When one member rejoices, all the members rejoice
When one member is honored, all the members are honored
One cannot do without the other and should not usurp the other
But each member should compliment the one body.

We salute all for your service
We salute all the past who have endeavored
For being soldiers with the shield of faith
The helmet of salvation, the sword of the spirit
The breastplate of righteousness in the army of God
Black women with scars on your backs, you are yet strong
Beyond all definition still defying place, time and circumstance
Black women, you are the salt of the earth, no happenstance
The Flavor Of The Universe and the clay of our race, our ace.

"When you control a man's thinking you do not have to worry about his actions. You do not have to tell him not to stand here or go yonder. He will find his "proper place" and will stay in it. You do not need to send him to the back door. He will go without being told. In fact, if there is no back door, he will cut one for his special benefit." Dr. Carter G. Woodson

Footsteps

Young men have visions while old men dream dreams
Sons, fathers, working together, a better world it seems
Sons of yesterday, men of today must make the leap
Sons of today, men of tomorrow, a better life you reap
To the elder man, your accomplishments, you made the difference
To the younger man, as you journey, to the old men, make inference.

Young and old men, many with stamina fought courageous battles
While fifteen to sixty millions enslaved in Africa, treated like cattle
Thirty five million suffered and died en route to various ports
Fifteen millions who suffered slavery in America, their lives out of sort
Some were scientists, doctors, astrologers, musicians, architects, preachers
Along with many missionaries, their skills made them by far great teachers
Be proud of where, your status, today in this America land
Negro, colored, black, African American, be proud and stand
No matter what others call you, it does not matter
But what you choose to answer to, you flatter.

Your right to citizenship was bought with a price by
Crispus Attucks, first African American to die, Boston Massacre, March 5, 1770, over 5, 000 Blacks fought for America's Independence, that's why
Nat Turner led 250 slave revolts and conspiracies, many he freed
Benjamin Banneker, mathematician, astronomer, freedom fighter indeed
Frederick Douglas, President, New England Anti-Slavery Society, a first
George Washington Carver, world famous chemist, invented usage for
    the peanut, sweet potato and soy bean, made his mark in time, proved his worth
Booker T. Washington organized the National Negro Business League,
Marcus Garvey, Universal Negro Improvement Assoc. many intrigue
James Weldon Johnson fought for the Dyer Anti-Lynching bill,
Eldridge Cleaver denounced black males' genocide, Vietnam, a great ill

Words 'N' Action

Martin Luther King Jr., Civil Rights Movement, he undertook
Adam Clayton Powell Sr., Congressman, the people, he never forsook
Benjamin E. Mays, educator & scholar who stood among the elite, the great
Like A. Philip Randolph, Founder of Pullman Porters' union, we appreciate
Huey Newton & Bobby Seale, Founders, Black Panther Party, history made
Jackie Robinson, Paul Robeson, Joe Louis, Malcolm X, a price they paid
Accolades to Louis Farrakhan, Al Sharpeton, Jesse Jackson, Andrew Young
Remember to pay homage to all those who are nameless and for now unsung.

The black man's blood, Footsteps built this country of thee
Let no one threaten, hurt you or cause you to flee
Salute your countrymen, with respect and honor due
For in return you command respect return to you
Salute one another with love, not with violence, hatred, guns
Taking the joy out of your life, and many others, lack fun.

Men, know the Footsteps you now trod through
Learn and teach your history, it's long overdue
Pass the torch on, love all your brothers, the same
Jews, Protestants, Muslims and Catholics, no matter the name
Recognize God in all you do and strive to be
Work while it is day, be diligent while you can see
When night comes no man can work, all is dark
Be sober in your doings and thinking, let all spark
Lest you may be mislead, misused and miseducated
And pretty soon you're worthless, and outdated.

"One who finds passion in living, lives well and contributes to all humankind."

African Americans

African American contributors are the unsung heroes of today
Omission from textbooks, no visible recognition, no say
African Americans, who know the truth, let it be known
Let your works, words be evidence of all that you've sown
Lack of African American recognition prompted a void filled
Dr. Carter G. Woodson, had an antidote that would fit this bill
As a Black history teacher, he was truly inspired
To create recognition week for Blacks' was it
This gave rise to Negro History Week in 1926
To much history to celebrate in one week
African American Heritage Month, we now bespeak:

African Americans are builders, landowners, rulers, inventors, name it
Inventors of simple household items to complex devices, our claim sits
1834 thru 1900, 341 inventions were patented by Blacks with much delight
Who didn't have enough money to buy patent, and sold them out right.

The first American clock was made by Benjamin Banneker
The gas mask and the traffic signal by Garrett Morgan
The electric street lighting, the first Bell telephone, Lewis H.   Latimer
An embalming technique by Pierre Cazenave
The ironing table, lawn sprinkler and steam dome by Elijah McCoy
The steam boiler furnace, incubator, automatic air brake, telegraph systems Granville T. Woods
A process for storing blood by Dr. Charles Drew
A cosmetic manufacturer, Madame C. J. Walker
Oil stove and refrigerator by J. Standard
Cotton chopper by W. H. Richardson
Lawnmower by J. A. Burr
Ironing board by Sarah Boone
Shampoo headrest by C. O. Bailiff
City Hall and Wall Street of New York, land near and about, owned by Blacks, hence, the Negro burial grounds
Madison Square Garden's land owned by Annie D'Angola
The two greatest canals, the Suez and Panama, built by Blacks

Words 'N' Action

The first pyramid in Egypt and the Step pyramid by Imhotep
Queen Nzingha of Africa reign, thirty plus years, defying European control.
Knowing your past, your future guide
If you don't know, learn as you stride
If you do know, then reach and teach
Knowledge is expensive but ignorance is deadly
No knowledge or wisdom, life's a wavering medley
Any child who knows why he or she lives
Lives well, lives with a purpose and gives
"It matters not where you are springing from,
But where you are springing to", a psalm!

"Dying doing what you were born to do is heavenly."

Daredevil Of The Sky

Bessie Coleman defied all odds in the sky
Soaring like an eagle, a master, she did fly
In the skies, she felt as free as a bird
The air, free of prejudice, not a word
Nicknamed Brave Bessie, her reputation grew
Who had the nerves of steel, fearlessly she flew
Wright brothers, airplane fifteen years invented
She dreamed of flying, her heart never contented
Born in Atlanta, Texas, January 26, 1892
Had twelve brothers and sisters, what a crew
With sharecroppers parents, she picked cotton
No education or school, until all cotton begotten
She loved school, walked four miles to attend
Had a whiz mind for numbers, in math ascend
Read books from the traveling library twice a year
About African American Heroes, she did cheer
Working for Whites, she longed for a way out
Believed she could do anything, had no doubt
At twenty free headed for Chicago, determined she went
As a manicurist at a barbershop , many ears she bent
Robert S. Abbott, publisher, Chicago Defender newspaper
One of America's first Black millionaires, a favorite capper
Her brother's war stories her dream reawakened
With dollars saved, a Paris flying school, she reckoned
1921, an international pilots' license obtained
Overnight fame, the spotlight, the elite she gained
Black pilot in the field of aviation, first on the fence
Two years before Amelia Earhart, no recognition hence
She was flying high, she fulfilled her dream
An overnight celebrity in America, she beam
Mastered daredevil dives, soared, she thrived
An eagle who knew no limits, she finally arrived
Everything she did, flying, lecturing, she excelled
Leaving a legacy of great stride and unparallel.

115

"Every man must decide whether he will walk in the light. "

Tuskegee Airmen, Righting the Wrong

From the start, decried as not having muscle coordination to fly
Taunted that Blacks couldn't cut it as fighter pilots, much decry
Became the most feared, respected pilots in World War II aircrew
So much so that White bombers pilots requested to fly with them anew
So impressive were there skills, trained at Tuskegee Army Air Field
One thousand from 1942-1946, many great pilots/bombers, did yield
While thousands of others worked as mechanics, support staff
Enduring much, dedicatedly served for this Country's behalf.

To the Tuskegee Airmen, the Congressional Medal given
The highest civilian honor, Righting the Wrong driven
Some say the recognition is sixty years long overdue
They helped to wind World War II, steadfastly like glue
Four hundred and fifty pilots flew combat missions, escorted bombers
Over Europe, North Africa, true nationalists, champion Voyageurs
Shot down 111 German planes, 15,000 combat missions
The only fighter group that never lost a bomber, their vision
Bomber pilots would specifically request their escort
Protected by African Americans, gave total support
After the war, arrival at home, racism they often faced
Saving the War, accomplishments ignored, seemingly erased
Three hundred members of this unit delightedly received
a bronze replicas of the award, each deserved and achieved
Some on walkers, in wheelchairs, nothing could withheld
Their appearance at this Ceremony, many with gratitude beheld
Recognition, Tuskegee Airmen's Legacy will forever display
The actual medal at the Smithsonian Institution, from this very day!

"A friend loveth at all times…" (Proverbs 17:17).

Leonard Hicks, The Ultimate Giver

There once was a man, Leonard Hicks
Whose personality reminded me of St. Nick's
When first he and I met
I couldn't understand yet
Why he came into my life
With his charm, cut like a knife
The first time he spoke
I thought what a joke
The more his persona insisted
The more every word, I resisted
He never ceased to enlist
My opinion, thoughts, a gist
Days, weeks, months, years went by
I thought, oh my, what a guy
We became almost like twins
Inseparable to the very end
Even on his dying bed, weak and frail
To the doctors, "this is my best friend", he yelled
Forever in my hearts he lives
Stayed life with a zest, had so much to give
In his last days, his memorial confirmed
This man has touched all with his wisdom and charm
The very young and even the old
He will truly be missed, adored, as the story goes!

About The Author

E.P. McKnight is a native of Moss Point, Mississippi. She attended Fordham University of Lincoln Center, New York City, New York where she obtained a Master of Science in Education.

As a writer, poet, producer, teacher, talk show host and actress, she has achieved much recognition and publication of her works in the Morning Song anthology, the Poetry Laureates and various local newsletters and magazines.

McKnight has spent countless hours writing inspirational expressions that have produced profound impact on her well diversified audience lives, making a difference in countless lives. Her expressions are concerned with everyday life situations and issues that bombard our psyche on a daily basis. Her work is sensitive, thought provoking, inspiring and educational.

McKnight is a member of Screen Actors Guild, American Federation of Television and Radio Artists and Actors' Equity Association and has had numerous roles in films, television and soap operas. She has performed in theaters throughout the North, South, West and East Coast regions as an actress/poet/playwright. She is a member of Toastmasters International.

Other works include Catch The Spirit 'N' Action, I Question America-Legacy of Mrs. Fannie Lou Hamer, Lessons of Black History Maker's 'N' Action and she is currently penning a self help novel and a numerous other theatrical projects. She also recorded SOULFood Poetry 'N' Action.

"**WORDS 'N' ACTION**", our favorite poems, **The Flavor of the Universe**, has encouraged me to continually making a difference in young lives, enlightening and encouraging each to do their very best, this makes my living not in vain. **Love Ministry**, love with all your heart, your neighbor as yourself, ministering each other by teaching and giving is our desire.
Lucille & Paul Goldsmith, My Parents

"**WORDS 'N' ACTION**" is divided into eleven categories representing life. She shares so much wisdom in her words which reflect our humanity and captures our joy, pain, fears, strengths, triumphs… and most important our spirituality and the power of God, love, faith and hope. Her poems are stirring, spiritual and touch the soul. The book is also an amazing tribute to her African American heritage and tradition while acknowledging and paying homage to God and all his Children…I am so blessed to know E.P. McKnight.   Jeanie Coggan, Teacher/Artist

"**Words 'N' Action** is very inspiring, thought provoking and spiritually illuminating. This book will help to stimulate and awaken you to the glory and wonder of being just you. Bless you and continue to give all of us some means for living."   Larinelle Lawhorn, Educator

"Each poem in **Words 'N' Action** has caused me to analyze and look at life and its' trials from a whole new perspective. I was encouraged, my faith was strengthening and life has a more focused purpose. It's recommended for all ages to read."   Jimmy Waddell, Actor & Writer

Words 'N' Action